SPIRITUAL
ENLIGHTENMENT
and INITIATION

Rudolf Joseph Lorenz Steiner
February 27, 1861 – March 30, 1925

FROM THE WORKS OF DR. RUDOLF STEINER

SPIRITUAL ENLIGHTENMENT
and INITIATION

Dr. Douglas J. Gabriel

Our Spirit, LLC
2024

OUR SPIRIT, LLC

P. O. Box 355
Northville, MI 48167

www.ourspirit.com
www.neoanthroposophy.com
www.gospelofsophia.com
www.eternalcurriculum.com

ISBN: 978-1-963709-04-9

Book Cover art by Charles Andrade at www.lazure.com

CONTENTS

Enlightenment Basics

The Lamrim is not the only Buddhist path that claims to offer the quickest path to enlightenment. Through the ancient teachings of the Bonpo religion, revealed through the Buddha Tonpa Shenrab Miwoche, there is a short path to enlightenment called Lojong, which builds its structure upon the Bonpo teachings of Dzogchen. Dzogchen is supposedly the easiest and quickest path to illumination leading to enlightenment taught in Bon and Nyingma Buddhist schools of philosophy. The steps to enlightenment are simple and threefold according to the Buddhist teacher Dawa Gyaltsen who said: *"Vision is mind. Mind is empty. Emptiness is clear light. Clear light is union. Union is great bliss."* Other Dzogchen teachings concerning the path to enlightenment indicate that once a teacher has prepared you, all that is left is to 'learn to see the light, hear the sounds, understand the words.' This can be accomplished without mantras, vajra tools, tantric deities, or other Buddhist spiritual practices. The Dzogchen master need only meditate on empty space, the Sun, or manifestations of the spirits through lights, sounds, and words.

It is our belief that Rudolf Steiner was fully aware of the translations of Tibetan texts that revealed these secret teachings to the West. Through his association with H. P. Blavatsky's *The Secret Doctrine*, Rudolf Steiner was well versed in Eastern teachings, particularly those Lamrim teachings that have filtered into Blavatsky's works from the Tibetan texts she called *The Golden Book of Precepts*. In fact, the Dalai Lama, who was incarnated at the time of Blavatsky, recognized her teachings as originating from Tibetan Buddhism. Rudolf Steiner took those teachings and modernized them and added the most important missing detail—the nature of the Cosmic Christ. Thus, the 'striving for enlightenment for the sake of all sentient beings' may be a path Christians can also walk. Therefore, studying Rudolf Steiner's *Knowledge of the Higher Worlds and Its Attainment* is a type of Lamrim, Lojang, Dzogchen, and path to enlightenment all rolled up into a Christian Cosmology. Rudolf Steiner uses that very word—enlightenment—to describe what he is teaching in this book.

We further believe that other writings and teachings of Rudolf Steiner also build upon the ancient wisdom of the past, especially Tibetan Buddhism. We find the evidence for this idea in his book, *The Stages of Higher Knowledge*, which builds upon what he revealed in *Knowledge of the Higher Worlds and Its Attainment*. In fact, part of the indications given by Rudolf Steiner in *The Stages of Higher Knowledge* are very similar to the teachings of Lojong. The Buddhist Lojong, in turn, is very similar to the Buddhist Lamrim teachings in that it shows how to work with the three higher spiritual vehicles called in the East by the Sanskrit terms: Manas, Budhi, and Ātman—Rudolf Steiner called them Spirit-Self, Life-Spirit, and Spirit-Human. They are the three higher spiritual vehicles found in the human nine-fold constitution, as given by Rudolf Steiner and called in theosophical teachings the 'Higher Triad.' Therefore, we thought it might be helpful to present the Lojong as another useful guide to the path of awakening the higher self.

We have previously discussed the nature of the path to enlightenment where we demonstrated many similarities between the Buddhist path of enlightenment and the path of Preparation, Enlightenment, and Initiation given by Dr. Rudolf Steiner in *Knowledge of Higher Worlds and Its Attainment*. We pointed out in that article that the Buddhist Lamrim stages of the path to enlightenment are expanded by Rudolf Steiner's contributions to these descriptions of ascension which refocus the spiritual path to be germane to our times. Any objective comparison between the two—the Lamrim and *Knowledge of Higher Worlds*—will show Rudolf Steiner's path to be 'new and improved' and completely cognizant of the ancient teachings concerning preparation, enlightenment, and spiritual initiation. As a matter of fact, Rudolf Steiner goes beyond the Enlightenment/Nirvāṇa (Spirit-Self—Manas) of Gautama Buddha and takes the next steps into Paranirvāṇa (Life-Spirit—Budhi) and Mahāparanirvāṇa (Spirit-Human—Ātman) to complete the ascension into the higher three spirit realms of the human ego ("I Am"). Rudolf Steiner also calls these realms 'Moral Imagination, Moral Inspiration, and Moral Intuition,' which are the higher forms of thinking, feeling, and willing.

In his book on enlightenment and initiation, *Knowledge of the Higher Worlds and Its Attainment* (GA 10), Rudolf Steiner defines and explains what he means by the word enlightenment:

> "Many believe that they must seek, at one place or another, the masters of higher knowledge in order to receive enlightenment. Now in the first place, whoever strives earnestly after higher knowledge will shun no exertion and fear no obstacle in his search for an initiate who can lead him to the higher knowledge of the world."

> "Spiritual Science gives the means of developing the spiritual ears and eyes, and of kindling the spiritual light; and this method of spiritual training: (1) *Preparation*; this develops the spiritual senses. (2) *Enlightenment*; this kindles the spiritual light. (3) *Initiation*; this establishes communion with the higher spiritual beings. It is not altogether necessary that the first of these three stages should be completed before the second can be begun, nor that the second, in turn, be completed before the third be started. In certain respects, it is possible to partake of enlightenment, and even of initiation, and in other respects still be in the preparatory stage. Yet it will be necessary to spend a certain time in the stage of preparation before any enlightenment can begin; and, at least in some respects, enlightenment must be completed before it is even possible to enter upon the stage of initiation."

"Enlightenment proceeds from very simple processes. Here, too, it is a matter of developing certain feelings and thoughts which slumber in every human being and must be awakened. It is only when these simple processes are carried out with unfailing patience, continuously and conscientiously, that they can lead to the perception of the inner light-forms. The first step is taken by observing different natural objects in a particular way; for instance, a transparent and beautifully formed crystal, a plant, and an animal. By sinking deeply into such thoughts, and while doing so, observing the stone and the animal with rapt attention, there arise in the soul two quite separate kinds of feelings. Out of these feelings and the thoughts that are bound up with them, the organs of clairvoyance are formed. The organs thus formed are spiritual eyes. The students gradually learns by their means, to see something like soul and spirit colors. The spiritual world with its lines and figures remains dark as long as he has only attained what has been described as preparation; through enlightenment this world becomes light. Every stone, every plant, every animal has its own particular shade of color. In addition to these there are also the beings of the higher worlds who never incarnate physically, but who have their colors, often wonderful, often horrible. Indeed, the wealth of color in these higher worlds is immeasurably greater than in the physical world."

"Once the faculty of seeing with spiritual eyes has been acquired, one then encounters sooner or later the beings here mentioned, some of them higher, some lower than man himself—beings that never enter physical reality. If this point has been reached, the way to a great deal lies open. Moreover, if a man has the strength and the endurance to travel so far that he fulfills the elementary conditions of enlightenment, he will assuredly seek and find the right guidance. Throughout his training he must continually increase his moral strength, his inner purity, and his power of observation. Without patience no genuine results can be attained."

We can see from Rudolf Steiner's definition and description of enlightenment that it is quite different than the Western esoteric student's understanding of the term. If, as Rudolf Steiner indicates, enlightenment should come before initiation, then enlightenment must be more common than one might think. Enlightenment—otherwise called Moral Imagination by Rudolf Steiner—is a step towards the spirit, not the final step or the 'be all and end all' of spiritual development. Enlightenment/Moral Imagination is the first of three steps to claim the higher spiritual nature of the human being—Moral Imagination/Spirit-Self, Moral Inspiration/Life-Spirit, and Moral Intuition/Spirit-Human. As Rudolf Steiner pointed out concerning the enlightenment of Buddha—which opened Buddha to the stage of Nirvāṇa—'it was a first step.' Buddha doesn't really teach his students how to get to Paranirvāṇa /Life-Spirit, or Mahāparanirvāṇa/Spirit-Human. It takes the embodiment of all three higher spiritual bodies to attain Buddhahood. During ascension through the Life-Spirit realm, the initiate must directly meet the Cosmic Christ, which is not usually understood to be part of Buddha's teachings. Thus, enlightenment for a Christian is only a prior stage before initiation and direct communion with higher beings.

Rudolf Steiner's view of enlightenment makes it plain that it is not the end goal—it is a rung on a tall ladder. In *The Gospel of St. Mark* (Lecture IV) Rudolf Steiner makes it perfectly clear that Buddha had a preliminary mission upon which Christ built further:

"The Buddha gave heavenly enlightenment to his pupils; Christ in His parables gave earthly enlightenment to the crowd."

Enlightenment for Rudolf Steiner and other Christians is much more attainable than the nebulous 'Nirvāṇa' and 'Enlightenment' of Gautama Buddha, as generally understood in Western esotericism. Enlightenment is simply a preliminary on the path of spiritual initiation, just as Preparation is a preliminary for Enlightenment.

In a lecture given by Rudolf Steiner in Berlin entitled: *The Inner Development of Man* (December 15, 1904, GA 53), we are given another description of enlightenment according to Anthroposophy:

> "The three stages of occult schooling are called Preparation (Catharsis), Enlightenment, and Initiation. During the first stage or level, man's being is prepared in such a manner as to allow the delicate structures of the soul to emerge. On the level of enlightenment man gains the means of perceiving in the soul realm, and through initiation he attains the faculty of expressing himself in the spirit realm."

In other words, preparation and enlightenment are pre-requisites to initiation, which is much more involved and requires more than the initial feelings of esteem, reverence, devotion, wonder, and awe developed in the preparation stage. Preparation prepares the chalice to be empty so that it can be filled with light, sound, words, and communion with the spiritual hierarchy. In Buddhism they call these the results of ascension—seeing lights, hearing sounds, understanding words of spirit beings from the hierarchical ranks above us (lights, sounds, rays, and the language of the spirit).

This preparation for ascension to become vessels who can see (lights), hear (sounds), and speak (rays/words) with the spirits beyond the threshold is necessary before the effects of initiation begin in the aspirant. These lights, sounds, and words are the methods whereby the spirit teaches the student. Rudolf Steiner calls them Imagination, Inspiration, and Intuition. He again defines enlightenment and initiation and describes these new senses of light, sound, and word in a lecture given in Berlin on December 15, 1904, entitled *The Inner Development of Man* (GA 53):

"Human individuality and that of cosmic beings is profound, unfathomably profound. One cannot achieve anything in this area save by patience, perseverance, and loving devotion toward the cosmic powers. These are forces which, like electricity in the external world, are powerful in the internal world. They are not only moral forces but forces of cognition. When the aspirant for enlightenment has become proficient in allowing such truths to dwell within his being for some time, if he has accepted them in thankfulness toward those who revealed them to him, then he will at last reach a special point, which sooner or later becomes available to everybody who has allowed tranquility and silence to come to fruition in his soul. This is the moment when his soul begins to speak, when his own inner being begins to perceive the great, eternal truths. Then, suddenly the world around him lights up in colors never seen before. Something becomes audible that he had never heard before. The world will radiate in a new light. New sounds and words will become audible. This new light and radiance ray toward him from the soul realm and the new sounds he hears come to him from the spirit realm. It is characteristic of the soul world that one 'sees' it. It is equally characteristic of the spirit world that one 'hears' it.

"The three stages of occult schooling are called preparation (catharsis), enlightenment, and initiation. During the first stage or level, man's being is prepared in such a manner as to allow the delicate structures of the soul to emerge. On the level of enlightenment man gains the means of perceiving in the soul realm, and through initiation he attains the faculty of expressing himself in the spirit realm."

Later in the same lecture, *The Inner Development of Man*, Rudolf Steiner makes it crystal clear that he is linking onto prior streams of esotericism when he releases mystery wisdom concerning preparation, enlightenment, and initiation. We should not be surprised that the content of Rudolf Steiner's teachings can also be found in ancient teachings of Tibetan Buddhism. Rudolf Steiner amplifies the material, updating it with Christianity and expanding the content to meet the needs of the modern spiritual aspirant but clearly connecting his instructions (rules) with past traditions:

"If self-development is sought for in this area, then part of it comes about through obedience to and observation of a great sum of rules and directions. The rules presented in this book were never made public in former times when, it must be understood, occult instruction was only taught in occult schools. Such instruction is still being given out in occult schools today because it is an intimate teaching process that takes place between two people. The rules that are put down in the book, *Knowledge of the Higher Worlds and its Attainment*, stem from ancient traditions. Because it is essential that the truth become known, the guiding spirits of evolution have given permission for the publication of these rules. Still, it is only possible to publish a certain amount. The rest had to be excluded because the most important rules can only be disclosed by word of mouth."

"What is found in *Knowledge of the Higher Worlds and Its Attainment* is apart from other books of instruction in that it is harmless. Only those guidelines are disclosed that cannot do damage to a person, even if they are not followed with patience and perseverance. They can do no harm even if a person practices them improperly. This had to be mentioned because the question has arisen as to why and by what authority a set of esoteric rules was published."

It is important to remember that the ancient traditions were given before the Mystery of Golgotha, the incarnation of Christ in Jesus of Nazareth, and thus need to be re-enliven for our times before they are fully useful in the direct perception of the spiritual world where Christ is appearing in the etheric realm as a 'Second Coming.' Enlightenment is not fully possible without encountering Christ in the etheric body of the human being and the Earth. Buddha did not teach about the Life-Spirit realm while he was incarnated on the Earth because it is the realm where Christ works in a most powerful way and reigns as king upon the throne of Heaven and Earth. Therefore, no enlightenment or initiation is complete without the understanding of the Cosmic Christ. Rudolf Steiner makes that clear in what he says about Christ and enlightenment in lecture six of his lecture course entitled: *Three Streams of Human Evolution, Augustus and the Roman Catholic Church, Rhetoric, Intellectual Soul and Consciousness Soul* (October 13, 1918, GA 184):

"Thus today, in the first third of the twentieth century, we are facing the approach of an important event for mankind. It is not an event now in the physical world, but an event that will come to men as a kind of enlightenment, reaching them before the first third of the twentieth century has run out. If the phrase is not misunderstood, one can call it the reappearance of Christ Jesus. But Christ Jesus will not appear in external life, as at the time of the Mystery of Golgotha, but will work in man and be felt supersensibly. He is present in the etheric body. Those who are prepared can constantly experience Him in visions, constantly receive His counsel; in a certain sense they can enter into a direct personal relation with Him."

The Stages of Higher Knowledge

In the preface to *The Stages of Higher Knowledge,* Marie Steiner tells us that in the 1904 *Lucifer-Gnosis* magazine articles appeared what later became the book, *Knowledge of the Higher Worlds and Its Attainment.* A continuation of these articles appeared under the title, *The Stages of Higher Knowledge.* They were intended, later on, to be formed into a second volume in continuation of *Knowledge of the Higher Worlds and Its Attainment.* In other words, the 'path to Enlightenment and Initiation' continued in *The Stages of Higher Knowledge* which describes the realm of Nirvāṇa (Spirit-Self/*Imagination*) that one attains through Enlightenment. Even beyond this realm of Enlightenment (Nirvāṇa-*Imagination*), Rudolf Steiner describes the realms of Paranirvāṇa (Life-Spirit/*Inspiration*), and Mahāparanirvāṇa (Spirit-Human/*Intuition*) which are also known as Manas, Budhi, and Ātman—or in the Buddhist traditions as Nirmanakaya, Sambhogakaya, and Dharmakaya. These three future 'bodies' of the human being are the redeemed and spiritualized astral, etheric, and physical bodies of the human being's constitution. They are realms where Angels, Archangels, and Archai live and work. These are the realms Rudolf Steiner calls Moral Imagination, Moral Inspiration, and Moral Intuition and are directly linked to the three higher egos of the human being—higher ego, true ego, comic ego.

Marie Rudolf Steiner tells us in the preface to the book *The Stages of Higher Knowledge,* that Rudolf Steiner has created a 'science of initiation':

> "Rudolf Steiner created a science of initiation in which henceforth every serious, morally striving human being can find the fundament that carries him; he will be able to take hold of the elements that sharpen his power of discrimination while new worlds open up to him. He need not grope uncertainly, having received enough instruction to guide him

until he finds the leader in the lands of spirit. This was not the case before Rudolf Steiner began his spiritual work. His deed is the science of initiation. Through it is revealed what lay hidden in the Mysteries of the ancient temples: namely, alongside the knowledge of cosmic evolution, the knowledge of the imminent descent of Christ, and what was sealed up in the Church: the redeeming deed of the liberation of mankind through the Christ and the gradual permeation of the ego of the individual with His power. Instead of personal guidance, the requirement now is that the human being find the way to the Ego of Mankind, to the Christ, through the forces of the Time Spirit [the Archangel Michael acting as our current Archai]. The consciousness of the individual human being is made mature for the acceptance of the higher ego force; self-consciousness is raised to Spirit-Self."

We find in *Knowledge of the Higher Worlds* the 'rules' for the path of enlightenment and the many helpful words of guidance needed to attain enlightenment. Rudolf Steiner carried those rules further in his other 'basic' books that were written as his testimony to spiritual enlightenment and initiation. You can find the golden thread of ancient mystery teachings throughout these books which clearly indicates to the reader that this wisdom is newly packaged, ancient secret teachings that Rudolf Steiner acquired through clairvoyant perception. No better demonstration of this reality is found than in *The Stages of Higher Knowledge*, which somewhat mirrors the secret teachings of Dzogchen—the Bonpo and Tibetan Buddhist's 'quickest path to enlightenment.' Just as *Knowledge of the Higher Worlds* is similar to the Tibetan Buddhist practice towards enlightenment called Lamrin, so too the book *The Stages of Higher Knowledge* is similar in form and content to the Dzogchen practice called Lojong. We will be able to see this first-hand by comparing some of the content of both Rudolf Steiner's books and the ancient practice of Lojong.

Below is a chronological list of Rudolf Steiner's basic books that reference spiritual development and the processes of preparation, enlightenment, and initiation. Reading them in the proper order will clearly show that Dr. Rudolf Steiner was laying down the new path to modern enlightenment and spiritual initiation.

- *Theosophy*, 1904 GA 9
- *Knowledge of the Higher Worlds and Its Attainment*, 1904, GA 10, (also known as: *The Way of Initiation, Initiation and Its Results*)
- *The Stages of Higher Knowledge*, 1905, GA 12
- *An Outline of Occult Science*, 1910, GA 13
- *The Spiritual Guidance of Mankind*, 1911, GA 15
- *A Road to Self-Knowledge*, 1912, GA 16
- *The Threshold of the Spiritual World*, 1918, GA 17
- *Three Stages of Anthroposophy—Cosmology, Religion, Philosophy*, 1922, GA 25

We present in the selections below, the content of *The Stages of Higher Knowledge* that are quite similar to the Lojong practice of enlightenment of the Bonpo and Nyingmapa Traditions of Buddhism. Rudolf Steiner published his book in Berlin in 1905 (GA 12), long before any of these Eastern practices were brought to the West or translated from the original.

> "In my book *Knowledge of the Higher Worlds and Its Attainment*, the path to higher knowledge has been traced up to the meeting with the two Guardians of the Threshold. The relation in which the soul stands to the different worlds as it passes through the successive stages of knowledge will now be described. What will be given may be called 'the teachings of occult science.'"

> "Before man enters upon the path of higher knowledge, he knows only the first of four stages of cognition. This stage is the one he occupies in ordinary life in the world of the senses.

Even in what is called science, we have to do only with this first stage of knowledge. In occult science this first stage of knowledge is called the "material mode of cognition."

This is followed by three higher stages, and there are still others beyond these. These stages of knowledge shall be described here before proceeding with the description of the "path of knowledge."

"Considering the ordinary method of scientific cognition, of apprehension through the senses as the first stage, we shall have to differentiate the following four stages:

1. Material knowledge,
2. Imaginative knowledge,
3. Inspirational knowledge – 'of the nature of will,' and
4. Intuitive knowledge."

"It must first be made quite clear what is significant in these different modes of cognition. In the ordinary sense, the knowledge of four elements are to be considered: (1) *the object*, which makes an impression upon the senses; (2) *the image*, which the human being forms of this object; (3) *the concept*, through which the human being arrives at a spiritual comprehension of an object or an event; (4) *the ego*, which forms for itself the image and concept based on the impression of the object."

"Therefore in 'material cognition' four elements have to be considered: sensation, image, concept, ego. At the next higher stage of knowledge, the impression made upon the outer senses, the 'sensation,' falls away. There is no longer any outer sensory object. Of the elements to which man is accustomed in ordinary knowledge there remains only the three: image, concept, and ego."

"Ordinary knowledge in a healthy individual creates no image and no concept when an object does not confront the outer senses. The ego then remains inactive. Whoever forms images of which the corresponding sensory objects do not actually exist lives in fantasy. But the occult student acquires this very faculty of forming images without the stimulus of external sensory objects. With him something else must take the place of outer objects. He must be able to form images although no object touches his senses. Something must step in to replace sensation. This something is Imagination. At this stage, images appear to the occult student in exactly the same way as if a sensory object were making an impression upon him. They are as vivid and true as sensory images, yet they are not of material, but of soul-spirit origin. Yet the senses remain entirely inactive. It is evident that the individual must first acquire this faculty of forming meaningful images without sense impressions. This is accomplished through meditation and through the exercises that have been described in the book, *Knowledge of the Higher Worlds and Its Attainment.*"

"The man confined to the sense world lives only among images that have reached him through the senses. The imaginative man has a world of images that he has received from a higher source."

"Careful training is necessary to distinguish illusion from reality in this higher image world. The capacity to decide what is 'real' and what is 'illusionary' in these higher regions can come only from experience, and this experience must be made one's own in a quiet, patient inner life. One must first completely stop up the springs of the fantastic; only thus can one come to Imagination. At this point it will be clear that the world that one has entered in this way is not only just as real as the world of sense, but much more real."

"In the third stage of knowledge, images no longer appear. The human being has now to deal only with 'concept' and 'ego.' Whereas at the second stage a world of images still surrounded one, remainder of the moment when a vivid memory instantaneously kindles impressions from the outer world, without oneself actually having such impressions, at the third stage not even such images are present. The human being lives wholly in a purely spiritual world. The pictures of Imagination have a vivacity and a comprehensiveness with which the shadowy memory pictures of the sensory world, and even the glittering and ephemeral physical world itself are not to be compared."

"Now the world of the third stage of knowledge. Nothing in the sensory world can even suggest its wealth and abundance. What was sensation at the first stage of cognition, imagination at the second, here becomes 'Inspiration.' Inspiration gives impressions, and the ego forms the concepts. If anything at all in the realm of sense can be compared with this world of Inspiration, it is the world of tone opened up to us by the sense of hearing. But now not the tones of earthly music are concerned, but purely 'spiritual tones.' One begins to 'hear' what is going on at the heart of things. The stone, the plant, and so forth, become 'spiritual words.' The world begins to express its true nature to the soul. It sounds grotesque, but it is literally true, that at this stage of knowledge one 'hears spiritually the growing of the grass.' The crystal form is perceived like sound; the opening blossom 'speaks' to one. The inspired man is able to proclaim the inner nature of things; everything rises up before his soul, as though from the dead, in a new kind of way. He speaks a language that stems from another world, and that alone can make the everyday world comprehensible."

"Lastly, at the fourth stage of knowledge Inspiration also ceases. Of the elements customarily observed in everyday knowledge, the ego alone remains to be considered. The attainment of this stage by the occult student is marked by a definite inner experience. This experience manifests itself in the feeling that he no longer stands outside the things and occurrences that he recognizes but is himself within them. Images are not the object, but merely its imprint. Also, inspiration does not yield up the object itself, but only tells about it. But what now lives in the soul is in reality the object itself. The ego has streamed forth over all beings; it has merged with them. The actual living of things within the soul is Intuition. When it is said of Intuition that 'through it [Intuition] man creeps into all things,' this is literally true."

"In ordinary life man has only one 'Intuition'—namely, of the ego itself, for the ego can in no way be perceived from without; it can only be experienced in the inner life. The perception of the ego is the prototype of all intuitive cognition. Thus, to enter into all things, one must first step outside oneself. One must become 'selfless' in order to become blended with the 'self,' the 'ego' of another being."

"Meditation and concentration are the sure means by which to approach this stage of cognition, like the earlier ones. Of course, they must be practiced in a quiet and patient way. Rich and vivid as are the worlds to which man may rise, yet they are delicate and subtle, while the world of sense is coarse and crude."

"Now when imaginative cognition approaches in man, part of the forces directed upon the body in sleep must be employed in another way. Through these forces are formed the spiritual sense organs that provide the possibility for the soul not merely to live in a higher world, but also to perceive it. Thus, the soul during sleep works no longer merely upon the body, but also upon itself. This work results from meditation and concentration, as well as from other exercises."

"Meditation, concentration, and other exercises bring it about that the soul withdraws for a time from its union with the sense organs. It is then immersed in itself. Its activity is turned inward. What is accomplished by immersion in the inner life bears fruit first of all in the state of sleep. When at night the soul is freed from the body, what has been stimulated in it by the exercises of the day works on. Organs take shape within it, through which it comes into connection with a higher environment, exactly as through the outer sense organs it had formerly united itself with the corporeal world. Out of the darkness of nocturnal surroundings appear the light phenomena of the higher world. Tender and intimate at first is this communion."

"Everything depends upon his learning to distinguish what is due to the ordinary world from what through its own nature presents itself as a manifestation from higher worlds. In a quiet, introspective mental life he must acquire this discernment. It is necessary first to develop a sense of the value and meaning of those intimate formations of the soul that mingle themselves with daily life as though they were 'chance impressions,' but that are really recollections of the nightly communion with a higher world."

"The lower nature of man must be fortified and made inaccessible to dangerous elemental influences. This can be brought about by the conscious cultivation of certain virtues. These virtues are set forth in the writings on spiritual development. Here is the reason why they must be carefully sought after. They are the following."

"First of all, the human being must, in a fully conscious manner, in all things, continually be intent upon the lasting, distinguish the imperishable from the transitory and turns his attention toward it. In all things and beings, he can suppose or discern something that remains after the transitory appearance has faded away. No one should neglect to do this, for no one who has not first made himself thoroughly familiar with the perishable aspect will detect the eternal in things. Then the heart must be fixed upon all that is valuable and genuine, which one must learn to esteem more highly than the fleeting and insignificant. In all feelings and actions, the value of any single thing must be held before the eyes in the context of the whole."

"Thirdly, Six Qualities should be developed:

1. Control of the thought world
2. Control of actions
3. Endurance
4. Impartiality
5. Trust in the surrounding world
6. Inner equilibrium."

Lojong Slogans for Enlightenment Training

Lojong is a mind training practice in the Tibetan Buddhist tradition based on a set of aphorisms formulated in Tibet in the 12th century by Chekawa Yeshe Dorje. This practice involves refining and purifying one's motivations and attitudes. The fifty-nine or so slogans that form the root text of the mind training practice are designed as a set of antidotes to undesired mental habits that cause suffering. They contain both methods to expand one's viewpoint towards absolute bodhicitta [enlightenment for the sake of all sentient beings].

Lojong, or mind training, is a core practice in all the lineages of the Tibetan tradition. They can perhaps best be characterized as a method for transforming our mind by turning away from self-centeredness and cultivating instead the mental habits that generate bodhicitta, the awakened mind that puts the benefit of others above all else. The teachings in it are more diverse than many people realize. The Lojong texts present a system for putting compassion into practice according to the teachings that originate with the Buddha himself and echo throughout the centuries.

The origin of Lojong, as a codified system, is generally attributed to Atisha, the eleventh-century Bengali master who came to Tibet and founded the Kadampa tradition and whose influence on all the Tibetan lineages was profound. From Atisha and the Kadampa masters who followed him, we have received a rich array of core Lojong texts that form the basis for the commentaries and teachings available today. Originally the Lojong teachings—often just collections of short sayings—were considered secret and were not widely disseminated.

While the core Kadampa Lojong texts are taught throughout the Tibetan schools, some schools gave them their own unique expression. There are two particular and very unique Nyingma presentations of Lojong in *The Root Text of the Seven Points of Training the Mind* by Chekawa Yeshe Dorje and *The Basic Path Toward Enlightenment* by Jamgon Kongtrul. In these masterful works, the authors present mind training from the core teachings familiar in all the well-known works and then introduces the Dzogchen-specific instructions, which are considered to be the quickest path to enlightenment in Bonpo and Tibetan schools of philosophy.

The Root Text of the Seven Points of Training the Mind, Chekawa Yeshe Dorje

and *The Basic Path Toward Enlightenment,* Jamgon Kongtrul

Point One: The preliminaries, which are the basis for dharma practice

1. Dharma exists by way of four ideas or Four Thoughts:

   • Maintain an awareness of the Preciousness of Human Life.

   • Be aware of the reality that life ends; death comes for everyone; Impermanence.

   • Recall that whatever you do, whether virtuous or not, has a result; Karma.

   • Contemplate that as long as you are too focused on self-importance and too caught up in thinking about how you are good or bad, you will experience suffering. Obsessing about getting what you want and avoiding what you don't want does not result in happiness, Ego.

Point Two: The main practice, which is training in bodhicitta
Absolute Bodhicitta

2. Regard all dharmas [teachings] as dreams. Anything spiritual is a dream. Although experiences may seem solid, they are passing memories.

3. Examine the nature of unborn awareness. Remember there is a state of awareness before even becoming aware of anything.

4. Self-liberate even the antidote to be free.

5. Rest in the essence of consciousness in the present moment.

6. In post-meditation, be a child of illusion.

Relative Bodhicitta

7. Giving and receiving alternate naturally. Sending and taking should be practiced alternately and should ride the breath.

8. Three objects, three poisons, three roots of virtue—The three objects are friends, enemies, and neutrals. The three poisons are craving, aversion and indifference. The three roots of virtue are the remedies: anti-craving, anti-aversion, and anti-indifference.

9. In all activities train with Lojong slogans.

10. Begin the sequence of giving and receiving with yourself.

Point Three: Transformation of Bad Circumstances into the Way of
Enlightenment

11. When the world is filled with evil, transform all mishaps into the path enlightenment. As the world fills up with evil, go find peace.

12. Drive all blames into one. Gather up all grievances into one.

13. Be grateful to everyone. Thank everyone.

14. Thoughts have no home. Thoughts keep going without stopping. Thoughts are lighter than light, completely insubstantial. Thoughts have no birthplace, thoughts are unceasing, and thoughts are not solid.

15. Four practices are the best of methods, accumulating merit, setting aside evil actions, offering to your demons and offering to your teachers.

16. Whatever you meet unexpectedly, join with meditation.

Point Four: Showing the Utilization of Practice in One's Whole Life

17. There are five heart strengths: determination, familiarization, positive seed, reproach and aspiration.

18. At death, release of consciousness is practicing the five strengths.

Point Five: Evaluation of Mind Training

19. All spiritual practice agrees on one point, lessen ego and self-absorption.

20. You know yourself better than anyone else knows you.

21. Keep a joyful frame of mind.

22. If you can practice even when distracted, you are well trained.

Point Six: Disciplines of Mind Training

23. Always follow three basic principles, dedication to practice, refraining from outrageous conduct, and developing patience.

24. Change your attitude but remain natural. Reduce ego attachment but still be yourself.

25. Don't talk about injured limbs, that is, take pleasure discussing defects in yourself and others.

26. Don't think ill of others and take pleasure thinking about their weaknesses.

27. Work with the greatest defilements first—work with your greatest obstacles first.

28. Abandon any hope of fulfillment. Rather than get caught up in how you will be in the future, stay in the present moment.

29. Abandon toxic food.

30. Be unpredictable and forget the slights of others.

31. Speak well of others.

32. Head off wrongdoing by others.

33. Head off avoidable disasters and shaming of others.

34. Carry your own burden and take responsibility.

35. Don't try to be the fastest—don't compete with others.

36. Do good deeds without twisting and scheming to benefit yourself.

37. Use these Lojong slogans as ways to decrease your self-absorption. Otherwise, gods

become demons.

38. Don't seek others' pain as the limbs of your own happiness.

Point Seven: Guidelines of Mind Training

39. All activities should be done with one intention.

40. Correct all wrongs with one intention.

41. Two activities: one at the beginning, one at the end.

42. Whichever of the two occurs, be patient.

43. Observe these two, even at the risk of your life.

44. Train in the three difficulties which are obstacles that arise too quickly for us to catch, when obstacles have arrived it's hard to know what to do about them, and obstacles keep coming back.

45. Adopt three principal causes, the teacher, the dharma, the sangha.

46. Pay attention that these three never wane, gratitude toward one's teacher, appreciation of the dharma (teachings), and correct conduct.

47. Keep these three inseparable—body, speech, and mind.

48. Train without bias in every way completely and wholeheartedly.

49. Meditate on whatever provokes resentment.

50. Don't be swayed by external circumstances.

51. This time, practice these main points, put others before self, dharma practice, and awaken compassion.

52. Interpret life's events correctly. Six things that may be misinterpreted are patience, yearning, excitement, compassion, priorities, and joy.

53. Be steadfast in your practice of these slogans. Don't vacillate in your practice of Lojong.

54. Train with all your heart. Train wholeheartedly.

55. Liberate yourself by examining and analyzing. Know your own mind honestly and fearlessly.

56. Set aside self-pity—don't wallow in self-pity.

57. Let go of jealousy—don't be jealous.

58. Ignore frivolity—don't be frivolous.

59. Expect no applause.

Eight Verses of Training the Mind
by Geshe Langri Thangpa

By thinking of all sentient beings

As more precious than a wish-fulfilling jewel

For accomplishing the highest aim,

I will always hold them dear.

Whenever I'm in the company of others,

I will regard myself as the lowest among all,

And from the depths of my heart

Cherish others as supreme.

In my every action, I will watch my mind,

And the moment destructive emotions arise,

I will confront them strongly and avert them,

Since they will hurt both me and others.

Whenever I see ill-natured beings,

Or those overwhelmed by heavy misdeeds or suffering,

I will cherish them as something rare,

As though I'd found a priceless treasure.

Whenever someone out of envy

Does me wrong by attacking or belittling me,

I will take defeat upon myself,

And give the victory to others.

Even when someone I have helped,

Or in whom I have placed great hopes

Mistreats me very unjustly,

I will view that person as a true spiritual teacher.

In brief, directly or indirectly,

I will offer help and happiness to all my mothers,

And secretly take upon myself

All their hurt and suffering.

I will learn to keep all these practices

Untainted by thoughts of the eight worldly concerns.

May I recognize all things as like illusions,

And, without attachment, gain freedom from bondage.

The Thirty-Seven Practices of All the Bodhisattvas
by Gyalse Tokme Zangpo

This poem was composed in Jewel Cave in Ngulchu by a teacher of scripture and reasoning for his own and others' benefit. He was a Dzogchen master who lived in the 8th century in the area of Zhangzhung. It was translated by Adam Pearcey in 2006.

The Thirty-Seven Practices of All the Bodhisattvas

You see that all things are beyond coming and going,

Yet still you strive solely for the sake of living beings —

To you, my precious guru inseparable from Lord Avalokita,

I offer perpetual homage, respectfully, with body, speech, and mind.

The perfect buddhas, who are the source of all benefit and joy,

Come into being through accomplishing the sacred Dharma.

And since this in turn depends on knowing how to practice,

I shall now describe the practices of all the buddhas' heirs.

The practice of all the bodhisattvas is to study, reflect, and meditate,

Tirelessly, both day and night, without ever straying into idleness,

In order to free oneself and others from this ocean of saṃsara,

Having gained this supreme vessel—a free, well-favored human life, so difficult to find.

The practice of all the bodhisattvas is to leave behind one's homeland,

Where our attachment to family and friends overwhelms us like a torrent,

While our aversion towards enemies rages inside us like a blazing fire,

And delusion's darkness obscures what must be adopted and abandoned.

The practice of all the bodhisattvas is to take to solitary places,

Avoiding the unwholesome, so that destructive emotions gradually fade away,

And, in the absence of distraction, virtuous practice naturally gains strength,

Whilst, with awareness clearly focused, we gain conviction in the teachings.

The practice of all the bodhisattvas is to renounce this life's concerns,

For friends and relatives, long acquainted, must all go their separate ways.

Wealth and prized possessions, painstakingly acquired, must all be left behind;

And consciousness, the guest who lodges in the body, must in time depart.

The practice of all the bodhisattvas is to avoid destructive friends,

In whose company the three poisons of the mind grow stronger,

And we engage less and less in study, reflection, and meditation,

So that love and compassion fade away until they are no more.

The practice of all the bodhisattvas is to cherish spiritual friends,

By regarding them as even more precious than one's own body,

Since they are the ones who will help to rid us of all our faults,

And make our virtues grow ever greater just like the waxing moon.

The practice of all the bodhisattvas is to take refuge in the Three Jewels,

Since they will never fail to provide protection for all who call upon them,

For whom are the ordinary gods of this world ever capable of helping,

As long as they themselves are trapped within samsara's vicious cycle?

The practice of all the bodhisattvas is never to commit a harmful act,

Even though not to do so might put one's very life at risk,

For the Sage himself has taught how negative actions will ripen

Into the manifold miseries of the lower realms, so difficult to endure.

The practice of all the bodhisattvas is to strive towards the goal,

Which is the supreme state of changeless, everlasting liberation,

Since all the happiness of the three realms lasts but a moment,

And then is quickly gone, just like dewdrops on blades of grass.

The practice of all the bodhisattvas is to arouse bodhicitta,

So as to bring freedom to all sentient beings, infinite in number.

For how can true happiness ever be found while our mothers,

Who have cared for us throughout the ages, endure such pain?

The practice of all the bodhisattvas is to make a genuine exchange

Of one's own happiness and wellbeing for all the sufferings of others.

Since all misery comes from seeking happiness for oneself alone,

Whilst perfect Buddhahood is born from the wish for others' good.

Even f others, in the grips of great desire, should steal,

Or encourage others to take away, all the wealth that I possess,

To dedicate to them entirely my body, possessions and all my merits

From the past, present and future—this is the practice of all the
bodhisattvas.

Even if others should seek to cut off my head,

Though I've done them not the slightest wrong,

To take upon myself, out of compassion,

All the harms they have amassed—is the practice of all the
bodhisattvas.

Even if others should declare before the world

All manner of unpleasant things about me,

To speak only of their qualities in return,

With a mind that's filled with love—this is the practice of all the
bodhisattvas.

Even if others should expose my hidden faults or deride me

When speaking amidst great gatherings of many people,

To conceive of them as spiritual friends and to bow

Before them in respect—this is the practice of all the bodhisattvas.

Even if others whom I have cared for like children of my own

Should turn upon me and treat me as an enemy,

To regard them only with special fondness and affection,

As a mother would her ailing child—this is the practice of all the
bodhisattvas.

Even if others, equal or inferior to me in status,

Should, out of arrogance, disparage me,

To honor them, as I would my teacher,

By bowing down my head before them—this is the practice of all the
bodhisattvas.

Even though I may be destitute and despised by all,

Beset with terrible illness and plagued by evil spirits,

Still to take upon myself all beings' ills and harmful actions,

Without ever losing heart—this is the practice of all the bodhisattvas.

Even though I may be famous and revered by all,

And as rich as Vaisravaṇa, the god of wealth himself,

To see the futility of all the glory and riches of this world

And to remain without conceit—this is the practice of all the
    bodhisattvas.

The practice of all the bodhisattvas is to subdue the mind

With the forces of loving kindness and compassion.

For unless the real adversary—my own anger—is defeated,

Outer enemies, though I may conquer them, will continue to appear.

The practice of all the bodhisattvas is to turn away immediately

From those things which bring desire and attachment.

For the pleasures of the senses are just like salty water:

The more we taste of them, the more our thirst increases.

The practice of all the bodhisattvas is never to entertain concepts,

Which revolve around dualistic notions of perceiver and perceived,

In the knowledge that all these appearances are but the mind itself,

Whilst mind's own nature is forever beyond the limitations of ideas.

The practice of all the bodhisattvas is to let go of grasping

When encountering things one finds pleasant or attractive,

Considering them to be like rainbows in the summer skies —

Beautiful in appearance, yet in truth devoid of any substance.

The practice of all the bodhisattvas is to recognize delusion

Whenever one is confronted by adversity or misfortune.

For these sufferings are just like the death of a child in a dream,

And it's so exhausting to cling to delusory perceptions as real.

The practice of all the bodhisattvas is to give out of generosity,

With no hopes of karmic recompense or expectation of reward.

For if those who seek awakening must give even their own bodies,

What need is there to mention mere outer objects and possessions?

The practice of all the bodhisattvas is to observe ethical restraint,

Without the slightest intention of continuing in saṃsaric existence.

For lacking discipline one will never secure even one's own wellbeing,

And so, any thought of bringing benefit to others would be absurd.

The practice of all the bodhisattvas is to cultivate patience,

Free from any trace of animosity towards anyone at all,

Since any potential source of harm is like a priceless treasure

To the bodhisattva who is eager to enjoy a wealth of virtue.

The practice of all the bodhisattvas is to strive with enthusiastic
    diligence —

The source of all good qualities—when working for the sake of all who
    live;

Seeing that even sravakas and pratyekabuddhas, who labor for
    themselves alone,

Exert themselves as if urgently trying to extinguish fires upon their
    heads.

The practice of all the bodhisattvas is to cultivate concentration,

Which utterly transcends the four formless absorptions,

In the knowledge that mental afflictions are overcome entirely

Through penetrating insight suffused with stable calm.

The practice of all the bodhisattvas is to cultivate wisdom,

Beyond the three conceptual spheres, alongside skillful means,

Since it is not possible to attain the perfect level of awakening

Through the other five paramitas alone, in wisdom's absence.

The practice of all the bodhisattvas is to scrutinize oneself

Continually and to rid oneself of faults whenever they appear.

For unless one checks carefully to find one's own confusion,

One might appear to be practicing Dharma, but act against it.

The practice of all the bodhisattvas is never to speak ill

Of others who have embarked upon the greater vehicle,

For if, under the influence of destructive emotions,

I speak of other bodhisattvas' failings, it is I who am at fault.

The practice of all the bodhisattvas is to let go of attachment

To the households of benefactors and of family and friends,

Since one's study, reflection, and meditation will all diminish

When one quarrels and competes for honors and rewards.

The practice of all the bodhisattvas is to avoid harsh words,

Which others might find unpleasant or distasteful,

Since abusive language upsets the minds of others,

And thereby undermines a bodhisattva's conduct.

The practice of all the bodhisattvas is to slay attachment

And the rest—mind's afflictions—at once, the very moment they arise,

Taking as weapons the remedies held with mindfulness and vigilance.

For once the kleshas [mental afflictions] have become familiar, they'll
  be harder to avert.

In short, no matter what one might be doing,

By always examining the status of one's mind,

With continuous mindfulness and alertness,

To bring about the good of others—this is the practice of all the bodhisattvas.

The practice of all the bodhisattvas is to dedicate towards enlightenment

All the virtue to be gained through making effort in these ways,

With wisdom that is purified entirely of the three conceptual spheres,

So as to dispel the sufferings of the infinity of beings.

Here I have set down for those who wish to follow the bodhisattva path,

Thirty-seven practices to be adopted by all the buddhas' heirs,

Based on what is taught in the sutras, tantras and treatises,

And following the instructions of the great masters of the past.

Since my intellect is only feeble and I have studied but a little,

This is not a composition likely to delight the connoisseurs,

Yet since I've relied upon the sutras and what the saints have taught

I feel these are indeed the genuine trainings of the buddhas' heirs.

Still, the tremendous waves of activity of the bodhisattvas

Are difficult for simple-minded folk like me to comprehend,

And I must therefore beg the indulgence of all the perfect saints

For any contradictions, irrelevancies, or other flaws this may contain.

Through whatever merit has here been gained, may all beings

Generate sublime bodhicitta, both relative and absolute,

And through this, come to equal Lord Avalokitesvara,

Transcending the extremes of existence and quiescence.

The poem above, *The Thirty-Seven Practices of All the Bodhisattvas,* is a 37-step path of training in Sutrayana that awakens the moral forces necessary to pass through the stage Rudolf Steiner calls 'Preparation' on the path to spiritual initiation. You may recognize many of Rudolf Steiner's core teachings in these pithy 'practices.' In the poem above it, *Eight Verses of Training the Mind,* you will find a transformed presentation of Buddha's Eightfold Path, laid out as advice for the soul of the aspirant. Rudolf Steiner often refers to the Eightfold Path in his path to enlightenment found in *Knowledge of the Higher Worlds.* All paths to enlightenment agree that moral development is needed at every stage of spiritual development. Mental training is secondary next to moral development. Rudolf Steiner tells us in *Knowledge of Higher Worlds and Its Attainment* that: "For every step in spiritual perception, three steps are to be taken in moral development."

The Tibetan Buddhist Lamrim and Lojong are excellent versions of ancient secret traditions from the Mystery Centers of Asia. They were the cutting-edge 'initiation science' of their time. Many elements of these practices are still applicable today and they are a comprehensive reminder of all that goes into spiritual Preparation and Enlightenment as the preliminary steps for further Spiritual Initiation. But in the final analysis, it is only through morality that the aspirant can reach enlightenment to commune with divine beings and attain knowledge of higher worlds.

Rudolf Steiner on Buddhism

The question of Rudolf Steiner's relationship to Buddha is too big to tackle in a short chapter because his indications about Buddha and Buddhism are copious and far-reaching. I provide many selections of Rudolf Steiner' indications concerning Buddha and Buddhism at the end of this chapter. Some of the indications of Rudolf Steiner about spiritual aspects of Buddha's life and mission are almost too incredible to imagine. The Bodhisattva, who became the Gautama Buddha, has a profoundly diverse spiritual expression that seems to have no end and sounds more like a legend or myth rather than a human being. From Siddhartha Gautama's past work on the planet Mercury, to his work currently on the planet Mars, Buddha's manifestations are at the heart of human development and hold a key to countless mysteries which work into our modern age.

Buddha's three turnings of the Wheel of Dharma in Sixth Century BC Northern India created 84,000 spiritual pathways into the teaching of enlightenment. This body of work, and its commentaries on the refined points of mental training, has created a variety of traditions that are almost impossible to comprehend throughout the different schools, practices, languages, and offshoots. Gautama Buddha has led the other Bodhisattvas, like: Skythianos, Zarathustra, Manes, Christian Rosenkreutz, and Elijah through the dark times of Kali Yuga and into the new age of light that is called Satya Yuga. Buddha taught and inspired Saint Francis and together they now work in the realm of Mars to bring peace and harmony to the beings who live there. Buddha over-lighted Saint John the Baptist and the Twelve Apostles and he donated his perfected astral body to Jesus of Nazareth in the manger. Buddha teaches us the path of the Bodhisattva to Buddhahood through his life, and illuminates the mission of his successor, the Maitreya Buddha, who is now a Bodhisattva continuing the Christian work of Gautama Buddha.

One might think that we are inflating the influence of Buddhism on Rudolf Steiner's path of spiritual development, but a careful examination of the Tibetan Buddhist's spiritual path to enlightenment, called the Lamrim, show many similarities with the paths to enlightenment described in Rudolf Steiner's *Knowledge of the Higher Worlds and Its Attainment*. Some of the content is similar and the overall tenor of the two paths highlight the same wisdom. That is not to say that Rudolf Steiner copied it; but, suffice it to say, there seems to have been an extreme focus on the teachings and influence of Buddha and his path to enlightenment. Rudolf Steiner is so impressed with elements of Buddha's teachings that he tells us: "It is a remarkable discovery of spiritual investigation that the most penetrating, most significant thoughts conceived in our present Epoch have proceeded from Gautama Buddha." This statement came from one of the leading Christologists of history who revealed the cosmic nature of Christ and filled in pieces to the 'missing years' of Jesus of Nazareth in his *Fifth Gospel*.

This frame of reference, uniting Tibetan Buddhism and Anthroposophy, may seem odd and out-of-place but the influences of Vedic, Hindu, Buddhist, and other Eastern schools of thought deeply affected the atmosphere of the Theosophical Society that Rudolf Steiner began his spiritual work within. He was the appointed leader for all questions on Christianity in the International Theosophical milieu, while Annie Besant and others were the official representatives of Eastern thought. This foundational difference in the two schools of thought in Theosophy forced Rudolf Steiner to have to withdraw from the Theosophical Society and create Anthroposophy. But this did not end Rudolf Steiner's ties with Eastern terms and Buddhist principles.

Rudolf Steiner went so far as to say: "And if we look at the whole of spiritual development in its progressive stages, we see that the Buddha, who sacrificed himself in the fire of love, is the inspirer of our Spiritual Science." This phrase may seem heretical to anthroposophists, but there is no doubt Rudolf Steiner wanted his followers to understand a great deal of Eastern wisdom as part of his Spiritual Science.

In the selections about Buddhism from Rudolf Steiner's works that we have provided below, Rudolf Steiner doesn't hesitate to spell out the limitations of Buddhism for our time as well as amazing marvels that tie Christianity and Buddhism together in most unusual ways. Rudolf Steiner brings these two seemingly different paths together when he indicates that Buddha's mission was to teach compassion and love, but Christ's mission was to be that love—to incarnate wisdom and love into one being. Rudolf Steiner tells us:—

"To bring the wisdom of love was the mission of the Bodhisattvas and of the Buddha; to bring to mankind the power of love was the mission of Christ."

Though the two paths, Anthroposophy and Buddhism, are both brilliant mind training systems, Rudolf Steiner considers Buddhism as a religion, belief, and practice to be inappropriate for modern times. The limitation of Buddha's way is that Gautama taught that only liberation from recurrent Earth lives can lead humanity to the realization of perfect freedom—essentially enlightenment or what he calls Nirvāna. This fallacy clearly overlooks the truth, beauty, and goodness found in the material world and the eternal aspects of love that do not deny 'Maya' is an illusion but also see the world as a garden to redeem—paradise regained. Christianity brings hope by conquering the fear and power of death, subsequently conquering Buddha's sorrows of illness, suffering, old age, and death. Christ's incarnation of love and wisdom was the fulfillment of Gautama's Buddhahood. Christ and Buddha still work together at this time in a most wonderful way because Buddha keeps evolving over time and does not stay tied and bound to the dogma and doctrine that was created from his teaching since he is no longer bound by repeated physical incarnations. Rudolf Steiner makes that distinction in his comparison between the two paths:—

> "The Buddha gave heavenly enlightenment to his pupils; Christ in His parables gave earthly enlightenment to the crowd."

The working together of Christianity and Buddhism seems to have taken hold strongly in the West, especially in America where many high lamas have come to live and teach. Buddhism, especially its ideas of karma and reincarnation have become American 'household words' and mix with Christians quite easily. It is commonly assumed that most young people in America believe in reincarnation and many other aspects of Eastern schools of thought. It is becoming commonly known that Buddhism is a sort of first stage to Christianity. If we pray, meditate, and get focused, then Christianity might have a chance to lead the next steps of spiritual development. Without Buddha's good work, Christ would have had a more difficult time with his message of love and forgiveness. As Rudolf Steiner once said: "Why could Christ work effectively? Because Buddha has spoken the truth."

Buddhism in the Light of Anthroposophy

Any comprehensive examination of Rudolf Steiner's views on Buddhism should include what the expert in Buddhism, Hermann Beckh, a student of Rudolf Steiner's and one of the original Christian Community Priests trained by Dr. Rudolf Steiner, has to say on the matter. Hermann Beckh, in *From Buddha to Christ* says of Buddha: "In Buddha, everything has an atmosphere of ending, in Christ, everything begins anew." This summarizes the decades of work I personally invested in understanding Rudolf Steiner's remarks about Buddha and Buddhism. If Tibetan Buddhist lamas are clairvoyant, then they should see Christ appearing in the etheric body of the

Earth and the human being, but they don't. Buddhism is waning in the area of current, direct perception of hierarchical beings who bring the newest revelations from the spiritual world. Buddhism is a living lineage, one that is old and unbroken but not timely with moral inspiration that brings love, freedom, and courage to modern ethical considerations. Buddhism is frozen in time and basically 'not Christian,' denying the efficacy of Christ's active presence in the etheric realm, which is observable by highly developed initiates and clairvoyants.

It was the question about Christ's current whereabouts that I often presented to the many Buddhist teachers I studied under in three of the five schools of Tibetan Buddhism. I have been honored to call some of the highest lamas my dear friends. I asked lamas the same question repeatedly: "Where does the active nature of the Etheric Christ fit into your cosmological system? Which deity represents Christ?" In general, they all denied Christ but then told me about Vishnu, Avalokiteshvara, Chenrezig, Tvashtar, Vishvakarma, Brahma, Vajrayogini, Kali, and many others who have similar characteristics. The same questions would be asked of Hindus, Krishnas, Jains, Bonpos, and others with the answers also denying Christ, but then telling of some solar hero who is the son, the highest god and goddess who came down to Earth to conquer death or a dragon or walk the path to the underworld and return alive. The Harvest King and Queen, the alchemical mysterious conjunction, the offering of the Grail Maidens, or the descent of New Jerusalem to meet the holy Bride are all allusions to the revelation of Christ, the Lamb who marries the Bride in New Jerusalem where the two trees intertwine and the spring of life rushes down in the four rivers of paradise.

Buddha's message is that he transcended the 'thirst for existence' and attained Nirvāṇa—the development of the Spirit-Self through the Manasic principle of moral, higher thinking. But the higher "I Am" of the Life-Spirit realm, through the Budhic principle, develops the even more refined forces of Moral Inspiration. This is Buddha's Paranirvāṇa.

Concerning my own integration of Rudolf Steiner's frequent references to Buddha and Buddhism's mind-training, I found it helpful to go back to Rudolf Steiner's basic books on initiation and stages of self-development. In these lectures and books, I often found similar content that is found in most Buddhist practices. Rudolf Steiner's and Buddha's paths of spiritual development both lead to realization, liberation, and enlightenment and systematically give advice, steps, prerequisites to the path, and the content of initiation rites leading to spiritual and moral development. Rudolf Steiner obviously arrived at the same conclusions that Buddha had arrived at, or perhaps Rudolf Steiner kept up with the Eastern teachers of Theosophy who were spreading esoteric Buddhism devoid of Christianity. Blavatsky's *Secret Doctrine* was taken from secret Tibetan texts she claims came from the Panchen Lama of Tibet. Rudolf Steiner was completely conversant in these teachings of Blavatsky and addressed refined points of difference between his beliefs and those of the Eastern school of Theosophy. Nevertheless, he was fully aware of the Tibetan Buddhist references in Blavatsky's works and especially the basic practice of Lamrim which was similar to the Tibetan Lamrim practices of Mahayana Buddhism.

Rudolf Steiner's familiarity with Blavatsky's claim that the *Stanzas of Dzyan* came from a Tibetan text entitled *The Book of Golden Precepts*, would have been a given. And the praise from the Panchen Lama about Blavatsky's book, *The Voice of Silence* would also be very familiar to Rudolf Steiner. One can easily see that the *Lamrim, The Voice of Silence*, and *Knowledge of Higher Worlds* have many similarities. Later in this book, we shall share examples of both the Lamrim practice and the Path of Enlightenment of Rudolf Steiner from *Knowledge of the Higher Worlds and Its Attainment*. These two paths are often coincident.

H. P. Blavatsky and the Panchen Lama

H. P. Blavatsky's teachings in *The Voice of Silence* are equivalent to the teachings on enlightenment found in the Tibetan Lamrim practices of the Panchen Lama. It is a path of initiation into higher knowledge. In *The Voice of the Silence,* Blavatsky takes the spiritual seeker through the Three Halls of the Probationary Path and a choice between the Two Paths—Open and Secret, the Secret being the path of the highest altruism of a Bodhisattva—and then on through the Seven Portals, which are the Paramitas or Perfections of Mahayana Buddhism.

The Seven Portals of *The Voice of Silence* are the gateways of virtue leading to the path of highest altruism and compassion. As Blavatsky says:—

> "To live to benefit mankind is the first step. To practice the six glorious virtues [Six Perfections] is the second."

According to Blavatsky, her book, *The Voice of the Silence* comes from *The Book of the Golden Precepts,* which forms part of the same series as that from which the *Stanzas of the Book of Dzyan* were taken, upon which her book *The Secret Doctrine* is based. She says that the *Book of the Golden Precepts* contains about ninety distinct treatises, three of these she translated into English for us in *The Voice of the Silence.*

In Mahayana Buddhism, we find works that serve as guides for our own training in the same noble ethics and compassion that Blavatsky urged us to practice in *The Voice of the Silence.* As Blavatsky says, "Thou canst not travel on the Path before thou hast become that Path itself."

The first installment of teachings said to be brought out from the secret commentaries was given by Blavatsky in *The Secret Doctrine.* She had made contact with teachers associated with a secret school, said by her to be 'attached to the private retreat of the Teshu-Lama,' i.e., the Panchen Lama.

Blavatsky wrote in a letter to her sister:—

> "*The Voice of the Silence*, tiny book though it is, is simply becoming the Theosophists' bible."

It has come to us as a translation of a secret work, unknown to the public. *The Voice of the Silence* was originally published in 1889 at about the same time the original Sanskrit text of the *Bodhicaryavatara* was also first published.

H. P. Blavatsky's *Secret Doctrine* is based upon *The Book of Dzyan* which is the first volume of the commentaries upon the seven secret folios of *Kiu-te*. Thirty-five volumes of *Kiu-te* for exoteric purposes and the use of the laymen may be found in the possession of the Tibetan Gelugpa Lamas in the library of any of their monasteries; and also, fourteen books of commentaries and annotations on the same by the initiated teachers. These fourteen volumes of commentaries are said to be "in the charge of the Teshu-Lama of Shigatse,"; i.e., the Panchen Lama. Blavatsky tells us in her *Collected Writings,* vol. XIV:—

> "Strictly speaking, those thirty-five books ought to be termed 'The Popularized Version' of *The Secret Doctrine,* which were taken from the *Book of the Secret Wisdom of the World*— containing a digest of all the occult sciences. These, it appears, are kept secret and apart, in the charge of the Teshu-Lama of Shigatse."

The known Books of *Kiu-te*, i.e., *rgyud-sde*, are the Buddhist tantras. It is further said that these "must be read with a key to their meaning, and that key can only be found in the Commentaries." The first volume of the known *Books of Kiu-te* contains the Kālacakra-tantra. The existence of the original *Stanzas of Dzyan,* the first volume of secret Senzar commentaries, was for many years denied by academic scholars and said to only exist as a figment of H. P. Blavatsky's imagination. They are most likely to be part of the lost *Mula Kalachakra* tantra texts.

The Ninth Panchen Lama of Tibet (1883-1937) officially endorsed *The Voice of the Silence* in 1927, pointing out that it comprises a part of the teachings of the Eastern Esoteric School and called it "the only true exposition in English of the Heart Doctrine of the Mahayana and its noble ideal of self-sacrifice for humanity." He also commented how important an esoteric Buddhist text it was and that "Madame Blavatsky had a profound knowledge of Buddhist philosophy."

In commenting on the 1989 centenary verbatim edition, the present Fourteenth Dalai Lama believes *The Voice of the Silence* "has strongly influenced many sincere seekers and aspirants to the wisdom and compassion of the Bodhisattva Path."

Buddha the Crown Jewel of India

It isn't hard to realize that Gautama Buddha was the crown jewel of both Vedic and Yogic wisdom rolled into a new understanding of the meaning of Brahman and the human Ātman. In fact, so much comes together in Buddha's new interpretation of ancient philosophy and spiritual practice that Rudolf Steiner tells us:—

> "It is a remarkable discovery of spiritual investigation that the most penetrating, most significant, thoughts conceived in our present epoch have proceeded from Gautama Buddha."

> *Buddha and Christ: The Sphere of the Bodhisattvas*
> Milan, September 21, 1911 (GA 130)

In *Esoteric Christianity and the Mission of Christian Rosenkreutz, The Christ Impulse in Historical Development*, Lecture II (Locarno, September 19, 1911, GA 130), Rudolf Steiner states that the most mature intellectual thinkers in Christianity were inspired directly by Buddha, mentioning Gottfried Leibniz (Jul. 1, 1646–Nov. 14, 1716), Friedrich von Schelling (Jan. 27, 1775–Aug. 20, 1854), and Vladimir Solovyov (Jan. 28, 1853–Aug. 13, 1900) as examples. This theme was taken up again in the aforementioned lecture *The Sphere of the Bodhisattvas*, (Milan, September 21, 1911, GA 130). Buddha's influence continued to manifest fruit even 500 years after his enlightenment under the bodhi tree when the second and third turning of the Wheel of Dharma provided new materials to advance his teachings. This great mystery is pointed at by Rudolf Steiner:—

The Gospel of St. Mark, Rudolf Steiner, VIII. Basel, September 22, 1912, GA 139

"'Under the Bodhi tree' means the same as 'under the fig tree.' From a world-historical point-of-view it was still the 'time of figs' in respect to human clairvoyance, that is to say it was possible to receive enlightenment as the Buddha did, under the Bodhi tree, under the fig tree.

"The disciples were to participate in this secret and know of it. Christ led them to the fig tree and told them the secret of the Bodhi tree, omitting to tell them, because it had no significance for them, that the Buddha was still able to find fruit on it.

"In the place of that scene of world history when the Buddha sat under the Bodhi tree stands the picture of Golgotha where another tree, the tree of the cross, is raised, on which hung the living fruit of the God-man revealing himself, so that from Him may radiate the new knowledge of the fruit of the ever growing tree that will bear fruit to all eternity."

Buddha was no mere philosopher or an ordinary religious founder but the esoteric teacher of the path of meditation and knowledge, and he placed openly before the world the path of meditation, which until then had been practiced in closed Yoga groups. Buddha himself emphasized the primary importance of this path in as much as the *Sermon of Benares* first proclaimed the noble Eightfold Path and only then the simple truth of suffering, which in the fourth of its stages again includes the Eightfold Path. Rudolf Steiner also recognized this fact in the way he worked the scheme of the Eightfold Path and its relationship to the sixteen-petalled lotus of the throat chakra; eight petals of which were developed in the past, leaving eight petals to be unfolded by the individual through the path of self-development as we move into the future. The Eightfold Path is also included as a specific reference in his presentation of the path of knowledge in *Knowledge of the Higher Worlds and Its Attainment*, although the many other things in this presentation are not exhausted within the scheme of the Eightfold Path.

The disciple of the Buddha longs to enter again into the pure Cosmic Light and leave the Earth to the darkness. While Christ, and whoever follows Him, goes right through the darkness in order that one day not only He, but with Him the Earth and the humanity of the Earth can be given back to the Cosmic Light, to the Primordial Light. On the other hand, the Buddha, and the path of Buddha, achieves only one part of the great task: it unites with the etheric element and leaves the Earth to the earthly element—*to death*. Consequently, he does not find the "I" that can only be fully discovered through its connection with Christ and the earthly element. For the etheric element by itself only knows the dissolution into the Cosmic Etheric.

The path of Buddha does not follow the Christian path in this Mystery of Metamorphosis and Resurrection. With Buddha we find miracles narrated of the super-earthly, spiritual accomplishments of the Perfected One, of siddhis (powers) and 'miracles of the Enlightened One'; but what the disciples experienced with the Risen Christ was much more. For Buddha's path leads only to Nirvāṇa, to dissolution into the Cosmic Astral and Cosmic Etheric, not to the Resurrection and Ascension of the Phantom Physical out of the earthly element. Nevertheless, we can learn from Buddha the tremendous thoughts of de-personalization of the cosmic experience. Here lies the greatness of Buddhism. This super-personal cosmic feeling we then incorporate into that striving, which not only reckons with personal destiny, but with the Earth and the future of the Earth. In such a way, the secrets of ancient Mysteries will become something much more powerful and grandiose if in the light of Christ, they find their renewal.

It is perhaps a good point to clarify early on the uniqueness of the Christ Event that came about through the Mystery of Golgotha. The best way is to let Rudolf Steiner explain this in his own words. To do this it was thought best to include a complete lecture; therefore it won't be surrounded by quotation marks, but rather it will be preceded and followed by a triangle.

$$\Delta$$

Initiation, Eternity and the Passing-Moment, Rudolf Steiner, Lecture II, Munich, August 26, 1912, GA 138

In these lectures we shall have to discuss important questions intimately related to spiritual life. We shall have to speak of what lies at the basis of so-called initiation and, after having indicated some of its secrets and laws, we must go on to speak of the significance of all that radiates out for life from initiation and initiates in the course of human evolution. We shall have to speak of all this in relation to what may be summed up in such contrasting ideas as eternity and the passing-moment, the light of the spirit and the darkness of life. Then, having considered the life of man from the point of view these ideas give, we shall return again to the power of initiation and the power of initiates. It is the principle of initiation, then, that on this occasion will be the limit of our studies.

Eternity—we need only touch on this idea to feel resounding in us something connected with the deepest longings of man's soul and with the highest aims of his endeavor. The passing-moment always brings before us all that surrounds us in life, that reminds us of the necessity to search in this passing-moment of our lives for what is able to give us a view into the land of our desire, into eternity. We only have to call to mind how Goethe introduced into his *Faust* the deepest secret of this his greatest poem, by making Faust say to the passing-moment. 'Tarry yet, thou art so fair!' and making him then confess that if such can become the soul's attitude, if it can so identify itself with this confession as to say to the passing-moment, 'Tarry yet, thou art so fair,' it must necessarily follow that Faust should own that he deserves to fall victim to Mephistopheles, the enemy of mankind on Earth. Thus, Goethe makes everything connected with the feeling that flows from the passing-moment the basic mystery of his greatest poem. It seems then that what we live in—*the passing-moment*—is in opposition to what we call eternity, for which man's soul must constantly long.

The light of the spirit! In all the anthroposophical studies we have pursued over the years, we have recognized that the striving after spirit light has the fundamental aim of leading man out of the darkness-of-life. Once more we feel how in *Faust*, one of the greatest poems in human evolution, a poet, wishing to portray a great and all-embracing soul, cannot but make it come forth out of the darkness-of-life. What is it that entangles Faust at the beginning of the poem? What envelops him? *It is the darkness-of-life.* How often have we to emphasize that so great is the force and power of this darkness over man—*that the spirit light, finding him immature, may so work upon him as not to illuminate but to dazzle and stun him.* So that the question may not only be, 'What is the way to the light of the spirit, where can it be found?' But rather, and above all, 'How must man tread the path of the soul that is able to lead him to the spirit light in the right way?'

These are only the guiding lines that should occupy us in these lectures. We have reached such a stage in our anthroposophical work that we need not develop our subject from the very start, but may connect it to some of the things already familiar to us.

When we meet the word, 'Initiation,' which is for us so intimately connected with the words eternity and spirit light, all the great men of whom we have heard in the successive Periods of humanity as initiates, become living in our souls. With them our souls call to life, too, the several Periods themselves, how they ran their courses, how men lived in them, and how the light streamed into humanity from both initiates and initiation temples in order to make possible what the impulses, the essential driving forces of human evolution, have in all ages become. It would take us too far afield today to refer in detail to all that happened in Earth evolution before the Atlantean catastrophe broke upon the face of the Earth, completely changing it. We can gain an adequate idea of what we are considering if we turn our gaze to Post-Atlantean times, remembering the particular configuration of the human being and his various aspects throughout the ages.

We will let our gaze sweep back over the characteristic civilization that followed immediately after the face of the Earth had been re-formed by the Atlantean catastrophe. We have often spoken reverently of all that in the first Post-Atlantean Period the great and holy teachers of mankind brought to that part of the Earth where later the Indian civilization was developed. We have remarked how the soul cannot but look up from below to the lofty spiritual teachings that came into the world at that time, through certain human individualities who still bore within them all the inward greatness of those men who in the Atlantean Epoch had direct communion, which was no longer possible in later Periods of mankind, with the divine spiritual worlds. We have pointed out how the heritage of Atlantean wisdom, now accessible to the occultist alone, lived on in a Post-Atlantean form in the ancient holy teachers of the first Post-Atlantean Cultural Period. We have also pointed out how great and significant man finds all that then lived, to which, now, it is only the Akashic Records that bear witness, when he receives reflections of it in Indian, or any other Oriental literature. The moral and spiritual sublimity contained in these writings as an echo of primeval spiritual teachings cannot be fully realized by present-day humanity insofar as external culture is concerned. Least of all can it be realized in the countries that have been prepared for their present external culture by what the various forms of Christianity have accomplished during the last centuries. Thus the soul felt directed upwards when it turned its gaze to all the greatness that, so dimly sensed today, has only come down to us as a faint echo of primeval spirituality. So, if man looks up to the old wisdom and remembers above all what has often been mentioned here, namely, that only in the seventh and last Periods of the Post-Atlantean Epoch will mankind again reach the point of drawing up out of the darkness of life the understanding of what once lived at the beginning of the Post-Atlantean Epoch and gave the impulse for human evolution—if we consider that mankind must mature to the last Period before it can feel and experience in itself what at that time was felt and experienced, then only shall we get a sense of how exalted must have been the initiation principle that gave the impulse to the ancient, holy, spiritual culture of mankind.

Then we see how, in the course of successive Periods, mankind, struggling for other spiritual treasures, other treasures of earthly life, seems to descend ever lower, how it takes other forms, but how, according to the needs of the age, great initiates give to men from the spiritual worlds what they require at any particular Period as an impulse for their culture. Then, before our vision, arises the Zarathustra culture that, if seen in its true light, entirely differs from that of the Holy Rishis.

We then see the Egyptian-Chaldean culture arise, and the ancient Holy Mysteries of Greece, to which we referred from a quite different aspect in our last lecture. Everywhere we see the light of the spirit shining down, according to the needs of the different Periods, into the darkness of life. If at the outset of our considerations, we ask what are our ideas of an initiate—it is obvious that at the beginning of these lectures only approximate ideas can be given of so vast a concept—we must first gather up much of all we have already heard in the anthroposophical field. We must be clear that for complete initiation it is necessary that man should not look out on the world from within his physical body in the usual way, by perceiving the world around him through his eyes and other sense organs, nor must he gain knowledge of this world or any other world around him through the intellect bound to the brain, nor through what he may call his sense of orientation. He must not form concepts about these worlds in the ordinary way. He must arrive at a stage in which, by means of what we may term 'the perceiving of worlds outside his physical body,' he develops something in his life of soul that maybe called a super-sensible spiritual body, having within it organs of perception, though of a higher kind, just as the physical body has eyes and cars and other organs of perception and understanding. 'One who can see worlds without using the organs of his physical body' can be given as an entirely explicit definition of an initiate. The great initiates, who gave man the important cultural impulses in the course of successive Periods, had attained in the highest measure independence of the sensory body, and use of another quite different in character.

I do not wish to say much that is abstract. Wherever possible I shall bring forward concrete examples, and today therefore I should like to illustrate this life outside the sensory body in a higher organization belonging to the soul and to illustrate it by means of the following example.

If one who has only gone a few steps on the way to initiation, realizes through self-observation what it is that he experiences in and of himself, he may say something like, 'One of the first things I experienced of myself is that I have within me, besides my physical body of flesh, a finer one that may be called an etheric body, which in Earth life is carried about with me just like the physical body.' Anyone making his first steps toward initiation realizes this at first in such a way that he feels within this body and experiences it just as, on another level, he feels what lives in his blood or nervous system, or in what arises from his muscular system. Such an inner feeling and experience is present, and it can exist also for the etheric body. It is then particularly useful for a student in the first stages of initiation to get to know the difference, or one might say the relationship, between the realization of himself, the experience of himself in his physical body, on the one hand, and on the other, in his etheric body. Man experiences himself in the etheric body in the same way as one is conscious of the blood or the beating of one's heart and pulse in the physical body.

To gain a clear idea of this we may consider the etheric body in connection with the physical body, in which one is more at home than in the body that one only succeeds in reaching by means of a journey into the spiritual. One may say to oneself, 'In my etheric body I have a part corresponding to my physical brain and to all that constitutes my head.' The head, the brain, is as though crystallized out of the etheric body, and so rests within it that it might be compared to a piece of ice floating in water—the water representing the etheric body and the ice, the physical body crystallized from the etheric body. An intimate connection is felt and experienced between what may be called the etheric part of the head or brain, and the physical brain itself. We then realize how we create our thoughts, how we form memory images within the etheric body, and how the physical

brain is only a kind of reflector; but we also realize how intimate
the connection of the brain is with the etheric body. This can
be experienced with especial force when one has to work hard
at tasks connected with the physical plane in the physical life,
when prolonged thought about things is necessary, and when
one must exert the physical body to bring up memory images
from the depths of life and to hold them together. In such a
process, the etheric body always takes a direct part, whether one
knows it or not. But inwardly connected with it is the physical
brain, and if this brain is tired out, fatigue is markedly felt in
the corresponding etheric part. We then notice something like
a block in what is experienced as the etheric part of the brain,
something like a foreign body, so that one can no longer get at
what one must know since mobility in the physical brain must
run parallel with mobility in the etheric body. You may then have
the distinct feeling that your etheric body never grows tired. It
would be able to gather up thought images to all eternity, and
bring to the surface all that you know. But before all this can
be expressed in the physical world, it must be reflected back,
and this the brain refuses to do. *For the etheric body never tires.*
Just because it can be continuously active, it notices the fatigue
of the brain all the more. One notices as it were the forces of
exhaustion produced by the brain, and when the brain goes to
sleep and falls into the torpor of fatigue, one might say, 'Now
you must stop, or you will be ill.' The etheric body cannot be
used up, but by giving the brain too much to do it is possible
indirectly to over tire it more and more, thus bringing about a
lifeless, deathlike condition. A living organism will not suffer
anything normally connected with it to be partially deadened
and brought into an abnormal state. Hence, out of a free resolve,
one must say, 'So that I may not kill part of my brain and leave it

to go on consuming itself, I must stop when I begin to feel it like something foreign inside me.'

That is what we experience when we try to find the relation between that part of the human or etheric body, which corresponds to the brain or head, and the physical brain or physical head itself. There is an intimate connection between them. In effect, the external life of the senses runs its course in such a way that it is impossible to break down what is parallel between the two. Therefore, if we want to express the relation, we may also say that in our head, especially in our brain, we have a faithful expression of the etheric forces, something that, in the external phenomena and external functions, gives us a really faithful image of the functions and processes in the corresponding etheric part.

It is different in the case of other organs of the human etheric body and the corresponding physical sense organs. These things are quite different. I will give you an example. Consider the hands. Just as there exists in the etheric body an etheric part corresponding to the head or brain, so there are etheric processes in the human etheric body corresponding to the hands. But the difference between the external physical hands and their tasks, and what lies at the basis of the corresponding etheric part is far greater than the difference between the physical head and its corresponding part in the human etheric body. What the hands perform has far more to do with the world of the senses and is much more a purely sensory function, while what is done by the corresponding etheric organs is only manifest in a small degree in what finds physical expression in the hands.

In order to describe the corresponding facts, I must, as is often the case, say things that appear grotesque and strange for physical experience, and for grasping physical observations in words. But what I say is fully in accordance with basic facts, and everyone who knows anything about these things will at once feel that they really are as I am obliged to describe them. They are the etheric parts corresponding to the physical hands. But apart from the fact that what corresponds to these etheric parts finds its expression in the hands and their movements, these etheric organs in the etheric body are true spiritual organs. The etheric organs expressed in the hands and their functions, work far more intuitively, more spiritually, and perform a far higher task than is accomplished by the etheric brain. Whoever has made progress in these matters will say that the brain with its etheric basis is in effect by far the least skillful of the spiritual organs man bears within him because as soon as he begins to bestir himself in the etheric part of the brain, he soon becomes aware of this foreign part of it.

The spiritual activities connected with the organs underlying the hands, but incompletely expressed in the hands and their functions, serve for a far higher, more spiritual kind of knowledge and observation. These organs can lead into the super-sensible world and can occupy themselves with our perception and orientation there. A spiritual seer may express this, somewhat surprisingly but accurately, by saying that the human brain is a most clumsy organ for research in the spiritual world, and that the hands, or the spiritual basis of the hands, are far more interesting and significant organs for gaining knowledge of the world, and are certainly far more skillful organs than the brain.

Not much is gained on the way to initiation by advancing from the use of the physical brain to a free use of the etheric brain. The difference is not great between what may be achieved through a purified, intuitive brain-thinking, and regulated spiritual working in the etheric spiritual counterpart of the brain.

The difference becomes much greater between what our hands accomplish in the world, and what can be done by the etheric part that is the spiritual basis of the hands, in the same way as the etheric brain is the spiritual basis of the physical brain. On the path of initiation not much development of the etheric brain is necessary since it is not a particularly important organ. But the etheric basis of the hands is connected with the activity of the lotus flower in the region of the heart, as you will learn in my book, *Knowledge of the Higher Worlds and Its Attainment.*

This lotus flower pours out its rays of force in such a way as to build up the organism that, at the stage at which physical man now stands, exists in an incomplete form in the hands and their functions. When we learn this fact and think of the great difference between the mere use of physical hands and all that we can acquire as regards the super-sensible world through the etheric organs underlying the hands—such far more skillful organs than those of the etheric brain—we gain a vivid conception of learning to experience initiation and all the enrichment that it means for man. We do not acquire much enrichment through the feeling that our brain radiates out to feel its etheric counterpart. This is the case, but it is not a really permeating and significant experience. The significant experience begins when one feels that other parts are also expanding and making contact with the universe. Though it may sound strange, it is true that the least skillful organ for spiritual investigation is the brain, since it is the least capable of development. On the other hand, entirely new perspectives are opened out when we consider other apparently subordinate organs.

Thus, there takes place a complete transformation of what man experiences in himself when he starts on the first steps toward the heights of initiation. It is necessary that one should bring this to consciousness, that one should grasp it as an inner transformation of the human personality, like the principle of development elsewhere in the universe; where one thing passes over into another—the latter being called, though perhaps not always appropriately, the more perfect as compared with the earlier. If we are clear how in the course of evolution one thing is transformed into another, how the seed of the plant is transformed and becomes leaves, flower and fruit, we can say that the human personality, too, experiences something of this kind; namely, what it is and what it can become through the methods given in *Knowledge of the Higher Worlds and Its Attainment*, which are the first beginnings of what may lead us right up to the highest regions of initiation. It is good—and you will see why— to arouse within us a living conception of how the men who are destined to become spiritual leaders in the course of time develop themselves inwardly, how all becomes transformed that is at first only germinal and appears so imperfect in man, like the hands in comparison with other organs. Outwardly, this transformation is not noticeable, but the inward change is all the more significant. Just as the outer world exists even for one who is blind and cannot see what is visible to others but only appears if the eye is there, so the world that is spiritual is present around us. But we have to bring to it what we can in order that the spiritual content of the world should approach us.

Now, in the various Periods of humanity there must stream into the course of evolution as impulses all that can be given through living oneself into the spiritual world. This is what was always behind everything proceeding from the mysteries, the initiation centers. A true idea of the course of human evolution may be gained by thinking of the great initiates as the real driving force, the real individuals, behind what is to be perceived externally. The connection between what these great initiates have to do and what happens externally in the World, often only becomes perceptible through anthroposophy or some other form of occultism. The external, purely historical knowledge of the learned only sees that human history, human evolution, is running its course; it does not see the driving forces behind it. In external history we follow what seems like a chain-of-phenomena, one link following another in a succession of external events. But that at certain points-of-the-chain impulses are entering from quite another world by way of initiation, this we only learn to accept through anthroposophical development.

Thus, anthroposophically we see the inmost center in the course of time and all that, fundamentally, gives to evolution its whole stamp and character. We perceive the various developments of religion as an out-streaming from the initiates. We perceive how the impulses flowing from the mysteries and initiation centers pass over into the general life of mankind.

Whoever regards the evolution of mankind in this way becomes, as a matter of course, free from any kind of a priori preference for a particular religion. This has always been the case with genuine occultism. It is one of the first requirements of initiation to divest oneself of all prejudices and preconceived feelings that grow up in a human soul when it incarnates into a particular religious system or community. In self-education one has to watch carefully that nothing remains in the soul that might give preference to any one religion. We must meet with absolute impartiality all that is contained in the various religions that, through initiation as impulse of development, has entered human evolution. As soon as there is any preference for a particular religion, something like an astral mist is formed through which no free vision is possible. Anyone who, by reason of an inclination that is a matter of course in ordinary life, harbors a preference in his soul for any religion, will never be able to understand other religions. Though he may not know it, he will perceive the predominance of one part of the contents of initiation and will never attain impartial knowledge of the other. Thus, for an occult view, it is obvious that one should confront without prejudice the various streams and impulses flowing from initiation. No one in studying a plant would give the flower preference over the root because he then would not be able to form an objective judgement of its whole structure. Just as little can a correct judgement of the inner content of one religious principle be gained if one is unable to observe other religions with complete impartiality.

In these lectures we shall be speaking of the demands the soul must make upon itself when taking the first steps toward initiation. I should like first to arouse a feeling of how initiation is related to life, and of how the various initiation centers and initiation impulses stand in regard to human evolution, particularly in the Post-Atlantean Periods.

Now occult investigation, in following up this course of human evolution, has a peculiar experience that can only be properly appreciated when such words as have just been spoken about the equal value of all religions are genuinely understood. When these ideas become a matter of course, something remarkable is experienced that will be increasingly better understood during the course of these lectures.

Let us turn our gaze to the initiates who give light to mankind as the ages go by. A man living primarily in the physical world, looking back on the initiates as historical and traditional figures, may say, 'Those are the great figures of world history.' When necessary, history has taken good care that as little as possible should be known of them. Although this may sound paradoxical, it is a good thing that humanity should know so little of Homer, for example, since it has not been possible for his image to be distorted by the learned as has been done in the case of other personalities. So will it be—*we may well long for this*—with Goethe when once he has become as unknown a personality as Homer is today! Man's soul then can look out into the external world at these personalities and see what they did there. Then he may himself take the first steps in initiation and become able to turn his gaze on the great figures of initiation such as Buddha or Zarathustra. He may be able to remember what Buddha or Zarathustra was to him in the world of the senses, what sort of impression he there received of these human individualities. Then, when some degree of spiritual light has dawned for him through initiation, he may ask, 'How does Buddha now appear to me, and how Zarathustra?' And he will say, 'I now have more knowledge of Buddha and Zarathustra. I know something I was not able to know in the world of the senses.' Such a man may then develop even further, until he comes to the stage when he will see better what these beings are as spiritual entities. One learns to know a Buddha, a Zarathustra, better the more one lives oneself into spiritual light until, when at last a certain limit is reached, it stops. That is one secret phenomenon, however, that has no need to be discussed further here. Suffice it to say that, *as higher worlds are approached, further knowledge may come to a stop*. This is the case as regards all initiates whom we meet in world evolution.

Now the spiritual student, who has not advanced too far, can easily be mistaken in these matters. That, however, is not of much consequence. It may happen that some human individuality, who in bygone ages stood high as a spiritual seer, on being reincarnated later, seems to have descended from his former spiritual heights. But the truth is simply that there are certain connections in human evolution where those who have already been initiates, are reincarnated as non-initiates because time-conditions call for them to accomplish certain deeds for which their initiation, latent during one or more incarnations, may work in some special way. Mistakes may easily arise about such individuals as they appear to us here or there making their way in external life, and quite wrong ideas may be formed about them. But in the course of progress these mistakes have gradually to be corrected. On the whole, therefore, it is a fact that man's relation to the initiates is such that he learns to know them better as he himself ascends toward the light of the spirit.

In the successive Periods of human evolution, we find one remarkable phenomenon. I could give examples of what I have just told you of the confusing way in which initiates on reincarnating sometimes appear to have come down from their heights. You would probably be much surprised if I told you, for instance, in what way Dante was reincarnated in the nineteenth century. But it is not my task here to discuss further this result of my own investigation and what was established for me. Rather have I to bring forward with strong proof the things known to everyone conversant with occultism, letting everything else recede into the background and stating nothing that is not generally recognized where genuine occultism is upheld.

Now another remarkable phenomenon appears to us that can best be expressed by saying that we meet with a Being regarding Whom it would be senseless to say that He was initiated like other initiates. While through Him the principle of initiation stands before us in the world objectively and is there, yet it would be meaningless to speak of this Individuality as having been initiated on Earth like other initiates in the course of human evolution. I have often touched on this fact. A certain degree of misconception has arisen by understanding this fact as originating in specifically Christian prejudice. In reality it is not any kind of Christian prejudice; *but should be stated as the objective result of occult research.* This Individuality Who was not initiated like other initiates, of Whom it would be quite meaningless to speak as having gone through initiation like others, is Christ Jesus Himself. Let us again emphasize that, just as it is impossible to understand a scale if it is said that it should be suspended from two points instead of one since the one point constitutes its very nature—just as it would be impossible for a competent mechanic to maintain that a scale should be suspended from two or more points, *it would be equally impossible for any genuine occultist to maintain that our Earth evolution could have more than one fulcrum, more than one center-of-stability.* I have said that this is an objective result of occult research that may be recognized by anyone, be he Buddhist or Muslim.

Anyone who has made certain progress in occult development learns to know the initiates insofar as they are great personalities or have done great deeds. He learns to know them in the spiritual worlds as he ascends toward initiation, and the higher he rises the better he learns to know them. Let us take the example of a man who possibly had no opportunity in his earthly life to learn to know the Buddha and had never concerned himself about him. I know people who have entered deeply into the whole life of the Occident without having any idea of the Buddha. It might be said of them that in their bodily life in the physical world they never had anything to do with him. Or take someone who in his earthly life has never interested himself in the great leaders of the Chinese religion. Imagine men of this kind entering the super-physical worlds through initiation or, as in some of the cases I know, entering these worlds for the first time after physical death. They can then become acquainted with Buddha, Moses, and Zarathustra because they can meet them as spiritual beings and gain a real knowledge of them. If they want to gain knowledge of these personalities, the fact that they had no opportunity to do so on Earth is no hindrance. But it is quite different in the case of Christ. *I beg you to receive this as an occult fact.* Suppose a man had never in any of his incarnations established a relation with the Christ Being. That is a hindrance to him when, in order to find Christ in higher worlds, he is using his perceptive faculties in an ultra-physical world; for Christ cannot then appear to him in His true form. It is on Earth that it is essential to prepare for the vision and recognition of the Christ Being in higher worlds. This is the occult difference in the relation of man to other initiates. The Christ event is such that something specific becomes related to the actual physical evolution of the Earth in its most important phase, radiates down into the Earth's physical evolution and forms its center-of-gravity.

Now let us assume that the beings who live out their lives as human souls did not at first pay any attention to the Earth. It might be that something happened in the course of the world to make these souls say, 'We will take no notice of the Earth; why should we incarnate down there?' This is, of course, impossible but let us assume it for a moment.

Then, insofar as what belongs to the Earth is spiritual, these human souls would be able to experience it in the spiritual worlds, and all the great, sublime principles that were active in the initiates would there be visible to them. Were such a soul in the higher worlds to put the question to cosmic evolution, 'Of all the beings in the higher worlds I want to know the Christ, to learn to understand His world mission and His essential task,' then the answer would have to be, 'If you would know the Being Who is for us the Christ, then you must incarnate on Earth. You must in some way participate in the Mystery of Golgotha in order to enter into relation with the Christ Being.'

The Christ Mystery had to take place on Earth in accordance with cosmic law. The Earth is the stage where, in accordance with cosmic law, the Mystery of Golgotha has had to be enacted, and where the essential foundation has had to be laid for an understanding of the Christ. The understanding of the Christ that man gains on Earth is a preparation, on a different scale to any other preparation that takes place on Earth, for any vision and knowledge of this Being in the higher worlds. *Therefore, in the Christ Being the principle of initiation was lived out in quite a different way from that of other initiates.* They experienced a super-sensible world, indeed, sometimes profoundly, and gave the various impulses out of that world into the course of human evolution. But when they had experience of the higher worlds, when they were within them, they were out of their physical bodies. Though it did not require much effort on the part of high initiates to leave the physical body, though but a small step was necessary to issue from it into the fullness of spiritual facts, yet it is true that this transition from the physical body to the higher bodies has to be made. In the Christ Jesus we have the distinctive phenomenon that, in reality, in accordance with the principle of initiation—in accordance, that is, with what man needs in order to bring about initiation—*He never, during the whole three years He was living on Earth, deliberately left the physical body as is done in initiation.* He always remained within it. All that He brought into life and gave to the world during those three years He gave through His physical body. The other initiates gave what they had to give to mankind through their super-physical bodies. In

Christ we have the one and only individuality Who has given all that He gave, all that He said, all that went out from Him into human evolution, through His physical body and never indirectly through the higher bodies.

In ordinary consciousness this is experienced in such a way that the sense of it can be summed up by saying that in Christ we have a phenomenon that can be understood by the most primitive consciousness that anyone possesses through the body by means of which we speak in everyday life. Hence, the intimate, brotherly union with the Christ Individuality, the possibility of understanding the Christ Individuality without the aid of education, simply by means of original primitive human feeling; hence, the necessity for working up to a higher form of comprehension, if one wishes to understand the other initiates. Thus, what I have often emphasized in these last ten years is true.

In Christ we have a Being Whom the simplest mind can understand, although anyone who has raised himself to this higher comprehension will understand Him better. In Christ Jesus all that can be connected with a human body was present, spiritualizing the human body to the greatest possible extent, and working in the human body through Christ Jesus. The other initiates were not able to be so fully active while giving forth what was spiritual because they had always to go out of their physical body and return to it later in order to reveal what they had retained of the super-sensible world. Christ, however, always had to live everything out in the physical world through the physical body.

Such things must be taken into consideration if we would go into the true connections. Everything else is empty talk, as for instance, when it is discussed whether Christ or the other initiates stand higher. Nothing is gained by such classification; that is quite beside-the-point. The essential thing is to look into the connection between the beings. It is a matter of personal preference whether the founder of one religion is deemed 'higher' than another. That will not do much harm; men are always subject to such little weaknesses. The important thing is to realize wherein consists the actual distinction between the position of Christ and that of the other initiates in the world. We may then calmly allow people to say, 'I consider this or that individuality the higher on account of what he did.' When the difference I have described is understood, the distinction will also be understood between the impulses that have come into the world through the various initiates.

$$\Delta$$

In the Middles Ages the mystery of the Christian path of initiation (the "Way') contained in the *Gospels* was, in a certain sense, already known. For it was recognized how the whole earthly life and suffering of Christ was not only a physical event; but was, at the same time, a picture for what in the depths of the Mysteries had been experienced upon the path of initiation into the spiritual-etheric realms from times immemorial. Through the Washing of the Feet, Scourging, Crowning with Thorns, Crucifixion, Burial, this was spiritually experienced and recognized, as having its effect directly upon the physical body *thereby leading to the Resurrection*. The Christian stages of suffering became the stages of initiation, and they do not find any correspondence within Buddha's path of enlightenment. For what was not yet contained in Buddha's path to Nirvāṇa, was the renewal and transformation of the Earth that was first achieved through the Mystery of Golgotha and can be seen in the picture of New Jerusalem which is the ultimate future of the Earth itself.

It is only in the light of Christianity that the true nature of the impulse given by Buddha appears revealed in its full depth. It is Christianity that first sets up the balance between the downward-driving and the upward-leading forces. The Buddha-forces, as yet un-permeated by the Christ-forces, are in themselves an urge to escape from the world, to turn away from the world. But when they are permeated with the Christ-impulse, they can be united with those forces which lead man down too insistently and too deeply into the earthly realm and sub-nature—*the forces of evil connected with the 'fall' into matter*. Christ unites the downward-driving and the ascending forces, the hardening and the loosening forces, in such a way that they intermingle and are thereby mutually purified. The true substance of the "I Am" is first given by Christianity. Buddha brought to mankind the teachings of compassion and love; while Christ, brought to mankind the actual transformative power of love. Buddha left his *'teachings'* as a legacy to humanity; Christ performed his *Deeds as a transubstantiation of Earth evolution*. Buddha was a master of the word; for in his words, the rhythms of the cosmic processes resound in wonderful harmonies. On the other hand, Christ *is* the 'Word'; for His whole life and being was an expression of cosmic harmonies, not merely His spoken words, *but also His Cosmic Deeds*.

The Tibetan *Lamrim* Practice

The *Lamrim* practice is a Tibetan Buddhist textual form for presenting the stages in the complete path to enlightenment as taught by Buddha. All versions of the *Lamrim* are elaborations of Atiśa's 11th-century root text, *A Lamp for the Path to Enlightenment*. Atiśa's presentation of the doctrine later became known as the Kadampa tradition in Tibet. Tibetan Buddhists believe that the teachings of the *Lamrim* are based on the sutras (Sanskrit: *sūtra*, lit. 'string, or thread') that the Buddha taught and therefore contain the essential points of all sutra teachings in their logical order for spiritual practice.

The *Lamrim* was the first Tibetan text translated into a European language by Ippolito Desideri, a Jesuit missionary, who visited Tibet and made an extensive study of Tibetan Buddhism from 1716-1721. Desideri studied the *Lam Rim Chen Mo of Tsongkhapa*, and his manuscript describing Tibet was one of the most extensive and accurate accounts of Buddhist philosophy until the twentieth century.

The *Lamrim* in Tibet is the backbone of Kadampa Buddhism. *Lamrim* is a special set of instructions that include all the essential teachings of Buddha Shakyamuni arranged in such a way that all his Hinayana and Mahayana teachings can be put into practice in a single meditation session. Many great Kadampa teachers have said that it is far more important to gain experience of *Lamrim* than it is to attain clairvoyance, miracle powers, or high social status. If we gain deep experience of *Lamrim*, there will be no basis for these problems; we shall become completely free of suffering and attain the unchanging peace and happiness of enlightenment.

An Example of the Tibetan Seven Limb Practice—*Lamrim*

This *Lamrim* practice was created by the 14th Dalai Lama, (Tenzin Gyatso, is considered a living Bodhisattva emanation of Avalokiteśvara and leader of the Gelug school of Tibetan Buddhism):

Taking Refuge to Buddha, Dharma, Sangha

May I be a guard for those who need protection

A guide for those on the path

A boat, a raft, a bridge for those who wish to cross the flood

May I be a lamp in the darkness

A resting place for the weary

A healing medicine for all who are sick

A vase of plenty, a tree of miracles

And for the boundless multitudes of living beings

May I bring sustenance and awakening

Enduring like the Earth and sky

Until all beings are freed from sorrow

And all are awakened.

Lamrim Preliminaries

Buddha's Individual Stages of the Path

1. Faith (saddha)

2. Meditation (samadhi)

3. Realization (panna)

4. Liberation (vimutti)

Buddha's Four Noble Truths

1. The truth of suffering

2. The truth of the causes of suffering

3. The truth of cessation of suffering

4. The truth of paths to attain this state free of suffering through practicing ethics, concentration and wisdom.

Buddha's Eightfold Path

1. Right knowledge

2. Right intention

3. Right speech

4. Right action

5. Right earning

6. Right exercise

7. Right mindfulness

8. Right meditation

Developing the mind of enlightenment (Bodhicitta)
through the Lamrim entails:

1. The wish to become a buddha for the welfare of all sentient beings,

2. Knowing the advantages of the mind of enlightenment,

3. The way to develop the mind of enlightenment,

4. The seven-point (seven limb) instruction in seeing all sentient beings as your mother,

5. Instruction on how to exchange your self-interest for others' interest,

6. Training your mind after developing the mind of enlightenment using the six perfections.

Lamrim practice is the Bodhisattva-path, training the Six Perfections:

1. Generosity

2. Morality

3. Patience

4. Energy

5. Meditation

6. Wisdom

The Buddhist's Series of Causal Links—Must be Overcome One at a Time

1. Ignorance

2. Power forming existence

3. Sentient consciousness

4. Name and form

5. The six senses

6. Touch

7. The feelings

8. Thirsting desire

9. Laying hold of sensory existence

10. Becoming in sensory existence

11. Birth

12. Old age, death, sorrow, lamentation, suffering, sadness, despair

The Twenty-one *Lamrim* Meditations

There are twenty-one *Lamrim* meditations, which are usually practiced in a three-week cycle as a daily meditation practice:

- Our precious human life
- Death and impermanence
- The danger of lower rebirth
- Refuge practice
- Actions and their effects
- Developing renunciation for samsara
- Developing equanimity
- Recognizing that all living beings are our mothers
- Remembering the kindness of living beings
- Equalizing self and others
- The disadvantages of self-cherishing
- The advantages of cherishing others
- Exchanging self with others
- Great compassion
- Taking
- Wishing love
- Giving
- Bodhicitta
- Tranquil abiding
- Superior seeing
- Relying upon a Spiritual Guide

Rudolf Steiner's Path to Higher Worlds

Eventually, in my own spiritual progression, I carefully compared the Tibetan *Lamrim* seven-limb practice and the basic Buddhist practices of taking refuge with *Knowledge of the Higher Worlds*. This book of Rudolf Steiner's created the union of Christianity and Buddhism that he had indicated would need to happen in the future. My personal decades of working with the *Lamrim* practice merged with the decades of work studying Rudolf Steiner, Waldorf education, Anthroposophy, and many of its fields of newly enlivened work. Buddhism became for me a wisdom path of understanding, compassion, and love. But only Christianity could meet the needs of our time as the Second Coming of Christ in the etheric realm is happening before our spiritual eyes. Ancient Buddhist texts may be correct in describing the path to free yourself from the Wheel of Life; but often the Christian path consciously chooses to work in the Wheel of Life until the 'big boat' (Mahayana) carrying many people can come along in the process of Ascension. Compassion and love lead the initiate into accomplishing even more loving deeds—*that are given out of freedom*—not for the sake of the release from karma and repeated human incarnations.

All quotations below are taken from: *Knowledge of the Higher Worlds and Its Attainment*, by Rudolf Steiner (GA 10), unless otherwise noted. The selections below will demonstrate great similarities between *Lamrim* and Rudolf Steiner's Christian, Western path of esoteric training leading to enlightenment.

This System of Training has Always Existed

"As long as the human race has existed there has always been a method of training, in the course of which individuals possessing these higher faculties gave instruction to others who were in search of them. Such a training is called occult (esoteric) training, and the instruction received therefrom is called occult (esoteric) teaching, or Spiritual Science."

"These practical rules have no arbitrary origin. They rest upon ancient experience and ancient wisdom, and are given out in the same manner, wheresoever the ways to higher knowledge are indicated. All true teachers of the spiritual life are in agreement as to the substance of these rules, even though they do not always clothe them in the same words. As long as the human race has existed there has always been a method of training, in the course of which individuals possessing these higher faculties gave instruction to others who were in search of them."

"The methods by which a student is prepared for the reception of higher knowledge are minutely prescribed. The direction he is to take is traced with unfading, everlasting letters in the worlds of the spirit where the initiates guard the higher secrets."

"In ancient times, anterior to our history, the temples of the spirit were also outwardly visible; today, because our life has become so unspiritual, they are not to be found in the world visible to external sight; yet they are present spiritually everywhere, and all who seek may find them."

"Whoever seeks higher knowledge must create it for himself. He must instill it into his soul. It cannot be done by study; it can only be done through life."

"Now man himself forms these higher senses through the exercises indicated by Spiritual Science."

"The latter include concentration, in which the attention is directed to certain definite ideas and concepts connected with the secrets of the universe; and meditation, which is a life in such ideas, a complete submersion in them, in the right way. By concentration and meditation, the student works upon his soul and develops within it the soul-organs of perception."

"A teacher of Spiritual Science who gives advice or instruction will, at the same time, always explain to those striving for higher knowledge the effects produced on body, soul, and spirit, if his advice and instructions be followed. The one who devotes himself to the study of Spiritual Science should do so with full consciousness; he should attempt nothing and practice nothing without knowledge of the effect produced."

"Students will recognize in the conditions attached to the development of the sixteen-petalled lotus the instructions given by the Buddha to his disciples for the Path. Yet there is no question here of teaching Buddhism, but of describing conditions governing development which are the natural outcome of Spiritual Science. The fact that these conditions correspond with certain teachings of the Buddha is no reason for not finding them true in themselves."

"The many repetitions in the sayings of the Buddha are not comprehensible to people of our present evolutionary stage. For the esoteric student, however, they become a force on which he gladly lets his inner senses rest, for they correspond with certain movements in the etheric body."

"Devotional surrender to them, with perfect inner peace, creates an inner harmony with these movements; and because the latter are an image of certain cosmic rhythms which also at certain points repeat themselves and revert to former modes, the student listening to the wisdom of the Buddha unites his life with that of the cosmic mysteries."

Knowledge of Higher Worlds Preliminaries

The Four Fundamental Attitudes of Soul Necessary for Higher Knowledge

1. the path of veneration—reverence, religious awe, worship, adoration, homage

2. the path of devotion—inner life, humility

3. the path of knowledge—self-education, respect, thought-life

4. the path of truth—selfless, respect, vivid inner-life, spiritual life

The Three Stages

Spiritual Science gives the means of developing the spiritual ears and eyes, and of kindling the spiritual light through this method of spiritual training:

1. Preparation; this develops spiritual senses

2. Enlightenment; this kindles spiritual light

3. Initiation; this establishes communion with higher spiritual beings

The Four Inner Habits

1. Discrimination between truth and appearance

2. Correct estimation of the affairs of daily life

3. Practice of the six qualities

   - Control of Thought
   - Control of actions

- Perseverance
- Tolerance
- Faith
- Equanimity

4. Longing for liberation

The Four Noble Laws

1. All knowledge pursued merely for the enrichment of personal learning and the accumulation of personal treasure leads you away from the path; all knowledge pursued for growth to ripeness within the process of human ennoblement and cosmic development brings you a step forward.

2. Every idea which does not become your ideal slays a force in your soul; every idea which becomes your ideal creates within you life-forces.

3. Adapt each one of your actions and frame each one of your words in such a way that you infringe upon no one's free-will.

4. Provide for yourself moments of inner tranquility, and in these moments learn to distinguish between the essential and the non-essential.

The Six Subsidiary Exercises

Guidance in Esoteric Training from the Esoteric School, **Rudolf Steiner, 1904-1914, GA 245**

1. Control of thought aims to gain control over what you think

2. Control of will aims to gain control over your actions

3. Equanimity—the exercise of feeling—aims to be aware of your feelings, to weaken strong feelings and strengthen weak ones and to balance them all

4. Positivity aims to see the positive in addition to the bad and the ugly as thinking and feeling are combined

5. Open-mindedness aims to be always open to new experiences as feeling and willing are combined

6. Inner harmony: the sixth, in which the previous exercises need to be practiced in order to create harmony between thinking, feeling, and willing

The Six Basic Exercises

1. Generosity

2. Ethics

3. Patience

4. Joyful Effort

5. Concentration

6. Wisdom

The Six Required Attributes

1. Control of thought

2. Control of actions

3. Control of actions

4. Tolerance

5. Impartiality

6. Equanimity

The Eight-fold Path

1. Right Opinion—*Saturday*—Pay attention to your thoughts— Discover living thinking through mindfulness

2. Right Judgment—*Sunday*—Decide with care—Weigh thoughts carefully and gain inner security

3. Right Speech—*Monday*—Mindful speech—Speak words thoughtfully, with warmth and meaning

4. Right Deed—*Tuesday*—Care-filled deeds—Interest and compassion—Follow the forces of the heart

5. Right Standpoint—*Wednesday*—Careful composition of life—Live naturally and spiritually

6. Right striving—*Thursday*—Serving your surroundings—Become responsive and create coherent relationships

7. Right memory—*Friday*—Learning from life—Becoming strong through devotion to life

8. Right Mindfulness—*Every day*—Becoming one—Live meditatively—become essential

The Six Conditions for Initiation

1. The student should pay heed to the advancement of bodily and spiritual health.

2. The student should feel himself coordinated as a link in the whole of life.

3. The student must work his way upward to the realization that his thoughts and feelings are as important for the world as his actions.

4. The student must acquire the conviction that the real being of man does not lie in his exterior but in his interior.

5. The student must display steadfastness in carrying out a resolution.

6. The student must develop of a feeling of thankfulness for everything with which man is favored.

7. The student must regard life unceasingly in the manner demanded by these conditions.

The Four Insights of Development

1. Insight into his higher self

2. Insight into the doctrine of the incarnation of this higher being in a lower

3. Insight into the laws of karma

4. Insight into the existence of the great initiates

The Three Alternating States of Consciousness

1. Waking

2. Dreaming sleep

3. Dreamless sleep

The Ten Negative Qualities to Conquer

1. Anger

2. Vexation

3. Timidity

4. Superstition

5. Prejudice

6. Vanity

7. Ambition

8. Curiosity

9. Mania for imparting information

10. Making false judgments about others

New Sight and Hearing Organs in your Soul and Spirit

1. Persevere in silent inner seclusion

2. Close the senses to all that they brought you before your training

3. Reduce to absolute immobility all the thoughts which surge within you

4. Become quite still and silent within, wait in patience

The Practical Rules

[Buddha's 'truth of Suffering']
Rudolf Steiner: Inner Tranquility

[Buddha's 'cause of suffering']
Rudolf Steiner: The student must set aside a small part of his daily life in which to concern himself with something quite different from the objects of his daily occupation.

[Buddha's 'stopping suffering']
Rudolf Steiner: During these periods the student should wrest himself entirely free from his work-a-day life. His joys and sorrows, his cares, experiences, and actions must pass in review before his soul; and he must adopt such a position that he may regard all his sundry experiences from a higher point-of-view. Our aim in these moments of seclusion must be to contemplate and judge our own actions and experiences as though they applied not to ourselves but to some other person.

[Buddha's 'understanding the cause of suffering']
Rudolf Steiner: Thought after thought, each fraught with advantage to his whole life, flows into the student's outlook. They take the place of those that had a hampering, weakening effect. He begins to steer his own ship on a secure course through the waves of life—this calm and serenity reacts on the whole being. They assist the growth of the

inner being which leads to higher knowledge. For it is by his progress in this direction that the student gradually reaches the point where he himself determines the manner in which the impressions of the outer world shall affect him.

[Spiritual Soul/Consciousness Soul]
Rudolf Steiner: No outward forces can supply space to the inner man. It can only be supplied by the inner calm which man himself gives to his soul. Outward circumstances can only alter the course of his outward life; they can never awaken the inner spiritual man. The student must himself give birth to a new and higher man within himself. This higher man now becomes the inner ruler who directs the circumstances of the outer man with sure guidance. The student must develop the faculty of letting the impressions of the outer world approach one only in the way in which they determine; then only does the aspirant become the serious student. And only in as far as the student earnestly seeks this power can he reach the goal.

[Buddha's Nirvāṇa/Manas/Spirit-Self/Higher Self]
Rudolf Steiner: An inner light is shed over the whole external world, and a second life begins for him. Through his being there pours a divine stream from a world of divine rapture. This life of the soul in thought, which gradually widens into a life in spiritual being, is called by Spiritual Science, "Meditation" (contemplative reflection). This meditation is the means to supersensible knowledge.

[Buddha's Paranirvāṇa/Budhi/Life-Spirit/Christened Self]
Rudolf Steiner: When, by means of meditation, a man rises to union with the spirit, he brings to life the eternal in him, which is limited by neither birth nor death. Thus, meditation is the way which also leads man to the knowledge, to the contemplation of his eternal, indestructible, essential being; and it is only through meditation that man can attain to such knowledge. Gnosis and Spiritual Science tell of the eternal nature of this being and of its reincarnation.

[Buddha's Mahāparanirvāṇa/Ātman /Spirit-Human/Cosmic Ego]
Rudolf Steiner: In right meditation the path is opened. This alone
can revive the memory of experiences beyond the border of life and
death. Everyone can attain this knowledge; in each one of us lies the
faculty of recognizing and contemplating for ourselves what genuine
Mysticism, Spiritual Science, Anthroposophy, and Gnosis teach. Only
the right means must be chosen.

Steps in Esoteric Training

*The following 'steps' are free renderings of Rudolf Steiner's ideas
concerning esoteric training.*

There slumbers in every human-being faculties by means
of which, he can acquire for himself a knowledge of higher
worlds.

Man has it in his power to perfect himself and, in time,
completely to transform himself. But he can rise to this higher
training if he has previously undergone rigorous training in
devotion.

Reverence awakens in the soul a sympathetic power through
which we attract qualities in the beings around us, which
would otherwise remain concealed.

One person sails across the ocean, and only a few inward
experiences pass through his soul; another will hear the
eternal language of the cosmic spirit; for him are unveiled the
mysterious riddles of existence. We must learn to remain in
touch with our own feelings and ideas if we wish to develop
any intimate relationship with the outer world. The outer
world with all its phenomena is filled with splendor, but we
must have experienced the divine within ourselves before we
can hope to discover it in our environment.

In Spiritual Science everything depends upon energy, inward truthfulness, and uncompromising sincerity with which we confront our own selves, with all our deeds and actions as a complete stranger.

Through her resounding tones, the whole of nature begins to whisper her secrets to the student.

What was hitherto merely incomprehensible noise to his soul becomes by this means a coherent language of nature. And whereas hitherto he only heard sound from the so-called inanimate objects, he now is aware of a new language of the soul. Should he advance further in this inner culture, he will soon learn that he can hear what hitherto he did not even surmise. He begins to hear with the soul.

When these exercises are practiced in connection with the others already given, dealing with the sounds of nature, the soul develops a new sense of hearing. She is now able to perceive manifestations from the spiritual world which do not find their expression in sounds perceptible to the physical ear. The perception of the 'inner word' awakens. Gradually truths reveal themselves to the student from the spiritual world. He hears speech uttered to him in a spiritual way.

It is necessary that the student should lose none of his qualities as a good and noble man, or his receptivity for all physical reality. Indeed, throughout his training he must continually increase his moral strength, his inner purity, and his power of observation.

During the elementary exercises on enlightenment, the student must take care always to enlarge his sympathy for the animal and the human worlds, and his sense for the beauty of nature.

How enlightenment proceeds if the student rises, in the sense of the foregoing exercises, from the stone, the plant, and the animal, up to man, and how, after enlightenment, under all circumstances the union of the soul with the spiritual world is affected, leading to initiation—with these things the following chapters will deal, in as far as they can and may do so.

In my own world of thought and feeling the deepest mysteries lie hidden, only hitherto I have been unable to perceive them.

Anyone having reached this point of spiritual vision is the richer by a great deal, for he can perceive things not only in their present state of being but also in their process of growth and decay. He begins to see in all things the spirit, of which physical eyes can know nothing.

And therewith he has taken the first step toward the gradual solution, through personal vision, of the secret of birth and death. For the outer senses a being comes into existence through birth and passes away through death. This, however, is only because these senses cannot perceive the concealed spirit of the being. For the spirit, birth and death are merely a transformation, just as the unfolding of the flower from the bud is a transformation enacted before our physical eyes.

This golden rule is as follows: For every one step that you take in the pursuit of higher knowledge, take three steps in the perfection of your own character.

Here again is another important rule for the student: Know how to observe silence concerning your spiritual experiences.

By following this path, the student approaches closer and closer to the moment when he can effectively take the first steps of initiation. But before these can be taken, one thing more is necessary, though at first its need will be least of all

apparent; later on, however, the student will be convinced
of it. The would-be initiate must bring with him a certain
measure of courage and fearlessness. He must positively go
out of his way to find opportunities for developing these
virtues.

The seer is to behold the working of these forces and the march
of destiny. The veil enshrouding the spiritual eyes in ordinary
life is to be removed. But man is interwoven with these forces
and with this destiny. His own nature harbors destructive
and constructive forces. He must not lose strength in the face
of this self-knowledge; but strength will fail him unless he
brings a surplus on which to draw. For this purpose, he must
learn to maintain inner calm and steadiness in the face of
difficult circumstances; he must cultivate a strong trust in the
beneficent powers of existence.

The higher we climb the ladder of knowledge; the more do we
require the faculty of listening with quiet devotion.

Now, when the student begins his exercises, the lotus flowers
become more luminous; later, they begin to revolve. When this
occurs, clairvoyance begins. For these flowers are the sense-
organs of the soul, and their revolutions express the fact that
the clairvoyant perceives supersensibly. No one can perceive
the supersensible until he has developed his astral senses in
this way.

The functions of the body, the inclinations and passions of
the soul, the thoughts and ideas of the spirit must be tuned to
perfect unison. The body must be so ennobled and purified
that its organs incite to nothing that is not in the service of
soul and spirit. The soul must not be impelled through the
body to lusts and passions which are antagonistic to pure and
noble thought.

The development of the lotus flowers alone does not assure sufficient security in these higher worlds; still higher organs are necessary.

Thus, a preliminary center is formed for the currents of the etheric body. This center is not yet in the region of the heart but in the head, and it appears to the clairvoyant as the point of departure for movements and currents. No esoteric training can be successful which does not first create this center.

The object of this development is the formation of a kind of center in the region of the physical heart, from which radiate currents and movements in the greatest possible variety of colors and forms. The center is not a mere point, but a most complicated structure, a most wonderful organ. It glows and shimmers with every shade of color and displays forms of great symmetry, capable of rapid transformation. Other forms and streams of color radiate from this organ to the other parts of the body, and beyond it to the astral body, completely penetrating and illuminating it.

The center in the head, once duly fixed, is then moved lower down, to the region of the larynx. This is affected by further exercises in concentration. Then the currents of the etheric body radiate from this point and illumine the astral space surrounding the individual.

All things now acquire a new significance for him. They become as it were spiritually audible in their innermost self and speak to him of their essential being. The currents described above place him in touch with the inner being of the world to which he belongs. He begins to mingle his life with the life of his environment and can let it reverberate in the movements of his lotus flowers. At this point the spiritual world is entered.

His lower self is before him as a mirrored image; but from within this image there appears the true reality of his higher self. Out of the picture of his lower personality the form of the spiritual ego becomes visible. Then threads are spun from the latter to other and higher spiritual realities.

The esoteric knowledge must first be studied, so that this study becomes a preparation for clairvoyance.

At this stage of his esoteric development the student realizes, through personal inward experience, all that had previously appealed to his sense of truth, to his intellect, and reason.

He has now direct knowledge of his higher self. He learns how his higher self is connected with exalted spiritual beings and forms with them a united whole. He sees how the lower self originates in a higher world, and it is revealed to him how his higher nature outlasts his lower.

He can now distinguish the imperishable in himself from the perishable; that is, he learns through personal insight to understand the doctrine of the incarnation of the higher self in the lower. He learns to recognize the law of his life, his karma.

Now, the ego which creates this organ of perception does not dwell within, but outside the physical body, as already shown. The heart organ is only the spot where the individual man kindles, from without, this spiritual light organ. It is precisely through the heart organ that the higher ego governs the physical self, making it into its instrument. This founding of a spiritual home is called in the language of occult science 'the building of the hut.'

Rudolf Steiner's Ideas Concerning Buddha

Metamorphoses of the Soul, Volume I, Rudolf Steiner, Lecture VIII, *Buddha and Christ*, Berlin, December 2, 1909, GA 58 (Also published as: *From Buddha to Christ*)

"Ever since its foundation, the spiritual-scientific movement has suffered from being confused with all sorts of other tendencies and strivings of the present day. Particularly it is accused of trying to transplant certain eastern spiritual currents, especially that of Buddhism, into the culture of the West. Hence our subject today has a special relevance for spiritual research: we are going to consider the significance of the Buddhist religion on the one hand and that of Christianity on the other, from the standpoint of Spiritual Science. Those who have often attended my lectures here will know that we intend a study in the scientific sense, ranging widely over world-events from the point-of-view of spiritual life.

"Anyone who has thought at all seriously about Buddhism will know that its founder, Gautama Buddha, always refused to answer questions concerning the evolution of the world and the foundations of our human existence. He wished to speak only about the means whereby a man could come to a way of existence that would be satisfying in itself...

"The Buddha-legend brings out clearly enough, even if in a pictorial form, what the founder of Buddhism was aiming at. We are told that Gautama Buddha, the son of King Suddhodana, was brought up in a royal palace, where everything around him was designed to enhance the quality of life. Throughout his youth he knew nothing of human suffering or sorrow; he was surrounded by nothing but happiness, pleasure and diversions. One day he left the palace, and for the first time the pains and sorrows, all the shadow-side of human life, met him face to face. He saw an old man withering away; he saw a man stricken with disease; above all, he saw a corpse. Hence it came to him that life must be very different from what he had seen of it in the royal palace. He saw now that human life is bound up with pain and suffering.

"It weighed heavily on the Buddha's great soul that human life entails suffering and death, as he had seen them in the sick man, the aged man and the corpse. For he said to himself: "What is life worth if old age, sickness and death are inescapably part of it?

"These reflections gave rise to the Buddha's monumental doctrine of suffering, which he summarized in the words: Birth is suffering, old age is suffering, illness is suffering, death is suffering. All existence is filled with suffering. That we cannot always be united with that which we love—this is how Buddha himself later developed his teaching—is suffering. That we have to be united with that which we do not love, is suffering. That we cannot attain in every sphere of life what we want and desire, is suffering. Thus there is suffering wherever we look. Even though the word 'suffering,' as used by the Buddha, does not have quite the meaning it has for us today, it did mean that everywhere man is exposed to things that come against him from outside and against which he can muster no effective strength. Life is suffering, and therefore, said the Buddha, we must ask what the cause of suffering is.

"Then there came before his soul the phenomenon he called 'thirst for existence.' If there is suffering everywhere in the world then man is bound to encounter suffering as soon as he enters this world of suffering. Why does he have to suffer in this way? The reason is that he has an urge, a thirst, for incarnation in this world. The passionate desire to pass from the spiritual world into a physical-corporeal existence and to perceive the physical world—therein lies the basic cause of human existence. Hence there is only one way to gain release from suffering: to fight against the thirst for existence. And this can be done if we learn to follow the eight-fold path, in accordance with the teaching of the great Buddha. This is usually taken to embrace correct views, correct aims, correct speech, correct actions, correct living, correct endeavor, correct thoughts, and correct meditation. This taking hold of life in the correct way and relating oneself correctly to life, will gradually enable a man to kill off the desire for existence, and will finally lead him so far that he no longer needs to descend into a physical incarnation and so is released from existence and the suffering that pervades it. Thus the four noble truths, as the Buddha called them, are:—

1. Knowledge of suffering
2. Knowledge of the causes of suffering
3. Knowledge of the need to end suffering
4. Knowledge of the means to end suffering

These are the four holy truths that were proclaimed by the Buddha in his great sermon at Benares in the fifth or sixth century B.C., after his illumination under the Bodhi tree.

"Release from the sufferings of existence—that is what Buddhism puts in the foreground, above all else. And that is why it can be called a religion of redemption, in the most eminent sense of the word, a religion of release from the sufferings of existence, and therefore—since all existence is bound up with suffering—of release from the cycle of repeated lives on Earth.

"This is quite in keeping with the conceptions described in the first part of this lecture. For if a thought directed to the outer world finds only nothingness, if that which holds together the parts of anything is only name and form, and if nothing carries over the effects of one incarnation into the next, then we can say that 'true existence' can be achieved only if a man passes beyond everything he encounters in the outer sense-world.

"It would obviously not be right to call Christianity a 'religion of redemption' in the same sense as Buddhism. If we wish to put Christianity in its right relationship to Buddhism from this standpoint, we could call it a 'religion of rebirth.' For Christianity starts from a recognition that everything in an individual life bears fruits which are of importance and value for the innermost being of man and are carried over into a new life, where they are lived out on a higher level of fulfillment. All that we extract from a single life becomes more and more nearly perfect, until at last it appears in a spiritual form. Even the least significant elements in our existence, if they are taken up by the spiritual and given new life on an ever more perfect level, can be woven into the spiritual. Nothing in human existence is null and void, for it goes through a resurrection when the spirit has transformed it in the right way.

"It is as a religion of rebirth, of the resurrection of the best that we have experienced, that we should look on Christianity—a religion for which nothing we encounter is worthless, but is rather a building-stone for the great edifice that is to arise by a bringing together of everything spiritual in the sense-world around us. Buddhism is a religion of release from existence, while Christianity is a religion of rebirth on a spiritual level. This is evident in their ways of thinking about things great and small and in their final principles.

"If we look for the causes of this contrast, we shall find them in the quite opposite characteristics of Western and Eastern culture. The fundamental difference between them can be put quite simply. All genuine Eastern culture which has not yet been fertilized by the West is non-historical, whereas all Western culture is historical. And that is ultimately the difference between the Christian and the Buddhist outlooks. The Christian outlook is historical: it recognizes not only that repeated earth-lives occur but that they form an historical sequence, so that what is first experienced on an imperfect level can rise in the course of further incarnations to ever higher and more nearly perfect levels. While Buddhism sees release from earth-existence in terms of rising to Nirvana, Christianity sees its aim as a continuing process of development, whereby all the products and achievements of single lives shine forth in ever-higher stages of perfection, until, permeated by the spirit, they experience resurrection at the end of earth-existence.

"Buddhism is non-historical, quite in the sense of the cultural background out of which it grew. It turns its gaze to earlier and later incarnations of man and sees him in opposition to the external world. It never asks whether in earlier times man may have stood in a different relationship to the external world or whether in the future this relationship may again be different—though these are questions that Christianity does ask. So Buddhism comes to the view that man's relationship to the world in which he incarnates is always the same. Driven into incarnation by his thirst for existence, he enters a world of suffering; it matters not whether the world called forth this same thirst in him in the past or will do so in the future. Suffering, and again suffering, is what he is bound always to experience during life on Earth. So Earth-lives are repeated, and Buddhism never truly connects them with any idea of historical development. That is why Buddhism can see its Nirvana, its state of bliss, as attainable only by withdrawing from the ever-repeated cycle of lives on Earth, and why it has to regard the world itself as the source of human suffering. For it says that if we ever enter the physical world, we are bound to suffer: the sense-world cannot but bring us suffering.

"That is not Christian, for the Christian outlook is historical through and through. It recognizes that man, in being born again and again, faces an external world; but if these encounters bring him suffering, or leave him unsatisfied, deprived of an inwardly harmonious existence, this is not because earthly life is always such that man must suffer; but because he has related himself wrongly to the external world.

"Christianity and the *Old Testament* both point to a definite event, as a result of which man has developed his inner life in such a way that he can make his existence in the world around him a source of suffering. Suffering is not inflicted on us by the world we perceive through our eyes and ears, the world in which we are incarnated; humanity once developed something within itself which placed it in a wrong relation to the world. And as this is inherited from generation to generation, it is still the cause of human suffering today. In the Christian sense we can say that from the beginning of the Earth-existence human beings have not had a right relation to the outer world.

"This comparison can be extended to the fundamental doctrines of the two religions. Buddhism emphasizes again and again that the outer world is Maya, illusion. Christianity, on the contrary, says: Man may indeed believe that what he sees of the outer world is an illusion, but that is because his organs are so constituted that he cannot see through the external veil to the spiritual world. The outer world is not an illusion; the illusion has its source in the limitations of human seeing. Buddhism says: Look at the rocks around you; look where the lightning flashes and the thunder rolls—it is all Maya, the great illusion. Christian thinking would reply that it is wrong to call the outer world an illusion. No, it is man who has not yet found the way to open the spiritual senses—his spirit-eyes and spirit-ears, in

Goethe's words—which could show him how the outer world is to be seen in its true form. Christianity, accordingly, looks for a pre-historical event which has prevented the human heart from forming a true picture of the outer world. And human development through a series of incarnations must be seen as a means whereby man can regain, in a Christian sense, his spirit-eyes and spirit-ears in order to see the external world as it really is. Repeated earth-lives are therefore not meaningless: they are the path which will enable man to look at the outer world—from which Buddhism wishes to liberate him—and to see it irradiated by the spirit. To overcome the physical appearance of the world by acquiring the spiritual vision that man does not yet possess, and to dispel the human error whereby the outer world can seem to be only Maya—that is the innermost impulse of Christianity.

"In Christianity, therefore, we do not find a great teacher who, as in Buddhism, tells us that the world is a source of suffering and that we must get away from it into another world, the quite different world of Nirvana. Christianity presents a powerful impulse to lead the world forward: the Christ, who has given us the strongest indication of the forces that man can develop out of his inner life-forces that will enable him to make use of every incarnation in such a way that its fruits will be carried into every succeeding incarnation through his own powers. The incarnations are not to cease in order to open the way to Nirvana; but all that we can acquire in them is to be used and developed in order that it may experience resurrection in the spiritual sense.

"Herein lies the deepest distinction between the non-historical philosophy of Buddhism and the historical outlook of Christianity. Christianity looks back to a *Fall* of man as the source of pain and suffering and onward to a *Resurrection* for their healing. We cannot gain freedom from pain and suffering by renouncing existence; but only by making good the error which has placed man in a false relationship with the surrounding world. If we correct this error, we shall indeed see that the sense-perceptible world dissolves like a cloud before the Sun, and also that all our actions and experiences within it can be resurrected on the spiritual plane.

"*Christianity is thus a doctrine of Reincarnation, of Resurrection*, and only in that light may we place it beside Buddhism. This, however, involves contrasting the two faiths in the sense of Spiritual Science and entering into the deepest impulses of both…"

The Christ Impulse and the Development of the Ego-Consciousness, Rudolf Steiner, Lecture I, *The Sphere of the Bodhisattvas,* Berlin, October 25, 1909, GA 116

"Gautama Buddha was a Being who had always been able to incarnate in the earthly bodies of the various periods of civilization, without having had to use everything in this human organization. It had not been necessary for this Being to go through real human incarnations. Now, however, came an important turning-point for the Bodhisattva; it now became necessary for him to make himself acquainted with all the destinies of the human organization within an earthly body which he was to enter…

"…In his incarnation as Gautama Buddha he saw, in advance, the first germ of what was to arise in man as conscience, which will become greater and greater as time goes on. He was therefore able to re-ascend into the spiritual world directly after that incarnation; there was no need for him to go through another. What man will, in a certain sphere evolve out of himself during future cycles, Buddha was able to give in this one incarnation, as a great directing force. This came about through the event which has been described as the 'sitting under the Bodhi-tree.' He then gave forth—in accordance with his special mission—the teaching of compassion and love contained in the eightfold path. This great Ethic of humanity which men will acquire as their own during the civilizations yet to come, was laid down as a basic force in the mind of the Buddha who descended at that time, and from Bodhisattva became Buddha, which means that he really rose a stage higher, for he learnt through his descent...

"...When this Bodhisattva, who had never really incarnated, was 29 years of age, his individuality fully entered the son of Suddhodana. He then experienced the great human teaching of compassion and love...

"...When the Consciousness Soul (Spiritual Soul) has been fully developed, man will, by its means, gradually become sufficiently ripe to recognize of himself the great impetus given by Buddha. At a time when man had only developed the Intellectual Soul, it was necessary that Buddha should already have developed the Spiritual Soul. He had so to use the physical instrument of the brain that he was complete master of it; and this in quite a different fashion than could have been done by one who might have progressed in advance as far as the Graeco-Latin period of civilization. The Graeco-Latin brain would have been too hard for him to use. It would only have enabled him to develop the intellectual or mind (Mind in the sense of 'I have a mind to do a thing.') soul, whereas he had to develop the spiritual soul. For that he required a brain that had remained softer. He made use of the soul that was only to develop later, in an instrument that had been used by man in earlier times and had been retained by the Indian people. Here again we have a recapitulation: Buddha repeated a human organization belonging to earlier times, together with a soul-capacity belonging to times yet to come. The events that take place in the evolution of humanity are to this extent, of the nature of a necessity. In the 5th to the 6th century before our era, Buddha had the task of introducing the spiritual-soul into the organization of man. He, as a single individual, could not, however, take over the whole task of doing all that was necessary in order that the spiritual-soul might prepare itself in the right way from the 5th century onward. His own particular mission only comprised one part of that task: that of bringing to man the doctrine of Compassion and Love. Other teachers of humanity would have other tasks. This part of the Ethics of Humanity, the ethic of Love and Compassion, was first introduced by Buddha, and its vibrations still endure; but humanity must in future develop a number of other qualities besides these, as, for instance, that of thinking in forms of pure thought, in crystal-clear thoughts. It was no part of Buddha's mission to build up thoughts, to add one clear thought to another. His task was to form and establish that which leads man of his own accord to find the eight-fold path…

"So there had to be another Teacher of humanity having quite different faculties, one who carried down a different stream of spiritual life from the higher spiritual worlds into this world. To this other individuality was given the task of carrying down what is gradually showing itself, in mankind today, as the faculty of logical thought. A Teacher had to be found, able to carry down what makes it possible for man to express himself in forms of pure thought; for logical thought itself only developed as time went on. What Buddha accomplished had to be carried into the Intellectual-Soul or Mind-Soul. This Soul, through its position between the Sentient-Soul and the Consciousness-Soul or Spiritual-Soul, possesses the peculiar attribute of not having to recapitulate anything. The Old Indian Period will be repeated in the seventh, the Old Persian in the sixth, the Egyptian in our own; but just as the fourth Period stands alone, apart from the others, so does the Intellectual-Soul or Mind-Soul. The forces necessary for our intellectual faculties which only appear in the Spiritual-Soul, could not be developed in the Intellectual-Soul; although these were only to appear later, they had to be laid down in germ and stimulated at an earlier period.

"In other words: the impulse for logical thinking had to be given before the Buddha gave the impulse for Conscience. Conscience was to be organized into man in the fourth Period [747 B.C.-1,414 A.D.]; conscious, pure thinking was to develop in the Consciousness-Soul or Spiritual-Soul in the fifth Period [1,414 A.D.-3,574 A.D.]; but had to be laid down in the third Period of civilization [2,907 B.C.- 747 B.C.], as the germ for what we are evolving now. That is why that other Great Teacher had the task of instilling into the Sentient-Soul the forces which now appear as pure thought. It is therefore easy to see that the difference between this Teacher and the normal man was even greater than it was in Buddha. Something had to be aroused in the Sentient-Soul which did not as yet exist in any living man. Ideas or conceptions would not have helped to develop this; therefore although this Individuality had the task of laying the germ of certain faculties, he could not himself make any use of them. That would have been impossible. He had to employ other, quite different, forces.

"I explained this morning (in the second lecture on "Anthroposophy") that certain forces working through the power of vision on the Sentient-Soul, will at a higher stage become conscious forces, and will then appear in the form of thought. If that great Teacher-Individuality was able so to stimulate the

Sentient-Soul that the forces of thought could penetrate it, in somewhat the same way as life subconsciously penetrated it through the act of vision—without the least realizing it, that Teacher could then achieve something. This could only be done in one way. To stimulate the Sentient-Soul and instill into it, so to speak, the power of thought, this Individuality had to work in a very special way. He had to give his instruction, not in conceptions—but through music! Music engenders forces which set free in the Sentient-Soul something, which, when it rises into the consciousness and has been worked upon by the Spiritual-Soul [Consciousness-Soul], becomes logical thinking. This music came forth from a mighty Being, who taught through music. You will think this strange, and may perhaps not believe it possible, yet such was the case. Before the Graeco-Latin Period [747 B.C.-1,414 A.D.], in certain parts of Europe, there existed an ancient culture among those peoples who had remained behind as regards the qualities strongly developed in the East. In those parts of Europe the people were not able to think much, for their development had been of quite a different nature; they had but little of the forces of the Intellectual-Soul. Their Sentient-Soul, however, was very receptive to what proceeded from the impulses of a special kind of music, which was not the same as our music today. We thus go back to a time in Europe when there was what we might call an ancient 'musical culture'—a time when not only the 'Bards' were the teachers, as they were later, when these things had already fallen into decadence; but when a music full of enchantment passed through all those parts of Europe. In the third Period of civilization (i.e., the Egypto-Chaldean Period 2,907 B.C.- 747 B.C.) there was a profound musical culture in Europe, and the minds of those peoples who were waiting quietly for what they were destined to carry out later, were receptive in a

particular way to the effects of music. These effects worked upon
the Sentient-Soul in a similar way to that in which the thought-
substance works upon it through the eyes. Thus did music work
on the physical plane; but the sentient soul had the subconscious
feeling: 'This comes from the same regions as the Light.' *Music—
the song from the realms of Light!*

"Once upon a time there was a primeval Teacher in the
civilized parts of Europe—a primeval Teacher who in this
sense was a primeval Bard, the pioneer of all the ancient Bards
and minstrels. He taught on the physical plane by means of
music, and he taught in such a way that something was thereby
communicated to the Sentient-Soul, which was like the rising
and shining of a Sun. What tradition has retained concerning
this great Teacher was later on gathered together by the Greeks—
who were still influenced by him from the West as they were
influenced in a different way from the East. This was embodied
in their conception of Apollo, who was a Sun-God and at the
same time the God of music. This figure of Apollo dates back,
however, to that great Teacher of primeval times, who put into the
human soul the faculty which appears today as the power of clear
thinking.

"The Greeks also tell of a pupil of this Great Teacher of
humanity—of one who became a pupil in a very special way. How
could anyone become the 'pupil' of this Being?

"In those bygone times, when this Being was to work in the
manner just described, he was not, of course, encompassed in
the physical organization; he transcended that which walks the
Earth as physical man. A man with an ordinary Sentient-Soul
might have been receptive to the effects of the music; but he
could not have aroused them in others. A higher Individuality
had come down and was like the radiance of what lived in the

Cosmos outside. It became necessary, however, that in the fourth Post-Atlantean Period of civilization, in the Graeco-Latin Period, he should descend again—that he should descend to the human stage and make use of all the faculties that are in man. Yet, although he made use, so to speak, of all the human faculties, he could not quite descend. For, in order to bring about what I have described, he required faculties transcending those possessed by a human organization in the fourth Post-Atlantean Period. The effects of this music even then included what was to be found in the Spiritual-Soul; and it could not at that time have lived in an individuality organized only for the Intellectual-Soul. Hence, although incarnated in such a form, he still had to hold something back. His incarnation in the fourth Period was such, that although he completely filled the whole human form, yet he as man, dwelling within that form, had, as it were, something within him that extended far beyond it; he knew something of a spiritual world, but he could not make use of this knowledge. He had a soul which extended beyond his body. Humanly speaking, there was something tragic in the fact that the Individuality who had acted as a great Teacher in the third Period of civilization, should have had to incarnate again in a form in which his soul was to a great extent outside it—and yet that he could not make any use of this superior and unusual faculty of soul. This kind of incarnation was called a 'Son of Apollo'; because that, which had dwelt on Earth before, was reincarnated in a very complicated and not in a direct way. A Son of Apollo bore within him as soul what Mysticism designates by the symbol of the 'feminine' element; he could not bear all of it within him, because it was in another world. His own feminine soul element was itself in another world to which he had no access but for which he longed, because a part of himself was there. This marvelous inner tragedy of the reincarnated Teacher of former times has been wonderfully preserved in Greek Mythology under the name of 'Orpheus'—the name given to the reincarnated Apollo, or 'Son of Apollo.'

"This tragedy of the soul is represented in a marvelous way in the figures of 'Orpheus and Eurydice.' Eurydice was soon torn from Orpheus. She dwelt in another world; but Orpheus still had the power, through his music, of teaching the beings of the nether world. He obtained permission from them to take Eurydice back with him. But he must not look around him; for that would mean inner death;—at all events it would bring about a loss of what he formerly was and which he cannot now take into himself.

"Thus, in this incarnation of Apollo as Orpheus, we have again a sort of descent of a Bodhisattva—if we may use this Eastern term—to Buddha-hood. We might quote a number of such Beings who stand out from age-to-age as the great Teachers of humanity and who always had a very special experience at the time of their deepest descent. The Buddha experiences the bliss of inspiring the whole of humanity. That Bodhisattva, whose memory is preserved externally under the name of 'Apollo,' had an individual experience: he was to prepare the individuality, the quality of the Ego. He experiences the tragedy of the Ego; he experiences the fact that this Ego is, in the present state of man as regards this attribute of his, not entirely with him. Man is struggling up to the Higher Ego. That was foreshadowed for the Greeks by the Buddha or Bodhisattva in Orpheus.

"These particulars furnish us with a characterization of the great Teachers of humanity and we are then able to form a picture in our minds. If you summarize what I have said, you will find that I have all along been speaking of those Beings who formed the Sentient-Soul and the Spiritual-Soul [Consciousness-Soul] in a particular way as inner faculties—faculties which must draw

into man from within. As we are now surveying this one period
we can only for the moment consider two of these Beings, those
who formed the Sentient-Soul. But there are many such, for the
inner nature of man evolved gradually, stage by stage."

The Gospel of St. Mark, Rudolf Steiner, Lecture IV, Basel, September 18, 1912, GA 139

"The Buddha has the task of preserving the culture of the
Sentient-Soul from the previous, the Third Epoch, into the
Fourth. What the Buddha announces, and his pupils take up
into their hearts, is something destined to shine over from the
Third Post-Atlantean Period [Egypto-Chaldean Period 2,907
B.C.- 747 B.C.]—the Period of the Sentient Soul—into the Era of
the Intellectual Soul [Graeco-Latin Period 747 B.C.-1,414 A.D.].
In this way the Era of the Intellectual Soul, the Fourth Post-
Atlantean Cultural Period, could be warmed through by the glow
and the light of the teachings of Buddha; by what was brought
forth by the Sentient-Soul, permeated as it was by clairvoyance.
The Buddha gave heavenly enlightenment to his pupils; Christ in
His parables gave earthly enlightenment to the crowd."

Excursus on the Gospel of Mark, Rudolf Steiner, Lecture III, Berlin, December 19, 1911, GA 124

"We must realize that the entrance into that state which Buddha
and Buddhism describe as being 'under the Bodhi tree,' is
a symbolic expression for a certain mystic enhancement of
consciousness and opens a path by which the human ego can
enter into its own Being, its own deeper nature. This path, blazed
by Buddha in such an outstanding way, is a descent of the ego into
the abyss of its own human nature…

"This is the other way in which the leaders of mankind arose. In speaking of it we have described, in a deeper sense, what we have often considered before: the two great streams of civilization of Post-Atlantean times. After the great catastrophe of Atlantis one of these streams continued to spread and develop throughout Africa, Arabia and Southern Asia; the other, which took a more northerly course, passed through Europe and Northern Central Asia. Here these two streams eventually met. All that has come to pass as a result of this is comprised in our Post-Atlantean culture. The northern stream had leaders such as I have just described in Zarathustra; the southern, on the other hand, those such as we see in their highest representative in the great Buddha.

"If you recall what you already know in connection with the Christ Event you might ask:— How does the Baptism by John in Jordan now strike us? The Christ came down and entered into a human being—as Divine Beings had entered into all the leaders and founders of religions—and into Zarathustra as the greatest of these. The process is the same, only here it is carried out in its sublimest form: Christ entered into a human being. But He did not enter this human being in childhood. He entered it in its thirtieth year, and the personality of Jesus of Nazareth had been very specially prepared for this event. The secrets of both sides of human leadership are given us in synthesis in the *Gospels*. Here we see them united and harmonized. While the evangelists, Matthew and Luke preferably, tell us how the human personality was organized into which the Christ entered; *The Gospel According to Mark* describes the nature of the Christ, tells of the kind of Being he himself is. The element that filled this great individual is what is especially described by Mark. The *Gospels* of Matthew and Luke give us in a wonderfully clear manner a different account of the temptation from that given in the *Gospel of Mark*, because Mark describes the Christ who had entered into Jesus of Nazareth. Hence the story of the temptation has here to be presented as it occurred formerly in the childhood of such great persons: the presence of animals is mentioned and the help received from spiritual powers. So that we have a repetition of the miracles of Zarathustra when the *Gospel of Mark* states in simple but imposing words:—

'And immediately the Spirit driveth him into the wilderness (loneliness). And he was there in the wilderness with the wild beasts; and the angels (that is Spiritual Beings) ministered unto him.'

Mark (I:12-13)

The Gospel of Matthew describes this quite differently, it describes what we perceive to be somewhat like a repetition of the temptation of Buddha; this means the form temptation assumes at the descent of a man into his own Being; when all those temptations and seductions approach to which the human soul is liable.

"We can therefore say the *Gospels* of Matthew and Luke describe the path the Christ travelled when He descended into the sheaths that had been given over to him by Jesus of Nazareth; and *The Gospel According to Mark* describes the kind of temptation Christ had to pass through when He experienced the shock of coming up against His surroundings, as happens to all founders of religions who are inspired and intuited by Spiritual Beings from above.

"Christ Jesus experienced *both* these forms of temptation, whereas earlier leaders of mankind only experience one of them. He united in Himself the two methods of entering the spiritual world; this is of the greatest importance; what formerly had occurred within two great streams of culture (into which smaller contributory streams also entered) was now united into one.

"It is when regarded from this standpoint that we first understand the apparent or real contradictions in the *Gospels*. Mark had been initiated into such mysteries as enabled him to describe the temptation as we find it in his *Gospel*; the 'Being with wild beasts,' and the ministration of spiritual Beings. Luke was initiated in another way. Each evangelist describes what he knows and is familiar with. Thus what we are told in the *Gospels* are the events of Palestine and the Mystery of Golgotha; but told from different sides.

"In stating this I wish once more to put before you, from a point-of-view we have as yet not been able to discuss, how human evolution has to be understood; and also how we must understand the intervention into it of such individuals as are passing on from the evolution of a Bodhisattva to that of a Buddha. We have to understand that the main thing in the evolution of these men is not so much what they are as men; but what has come down into them from above. Only in the form of Christ are these two united, *and it is only when we realize this that we can rightly understand this form.* We can also understand through this the many inequalities that must appear in Mythical personalities."

The Gospel of St. Luke, Rudolf Steiner, Lecture IV, Basel September 18, 1909, GA 114

"In the fifth-sixth century before our Era there lived in India the great Bodhisattva whose mission it was to bring to humanity truths that were gradually to arise in humanity itself. He gave the impulse for this and thereby became Buddha. Hence, he does not again appear in an earthly body; he appears in the Nirmanakaya, the 'Body of Transformation'; but only as far as the etheric-astral world. The shepherds, being for the moment clairvoyant, see him in the form of the angelic host; for they are meant to behold in vision what is being announced to them. In his Nirmanakaya, the Buddha inclines over the child born to Joseph and Mary of the Nathan line—for a very special purpose.

"What the Buddha had been able to bring to humanity needed to be present in a mature form; it was difficult to understand for it came from great spiritual heights. If what Buddha had achieved hitherto was to become universally fruitful, it was necessary for an entirely fresh and youthful force to flow into it. He had to draw this force from the Earth by inclining over a human child from whom he could receive all the youthful forces from the astral sheath when it was detached. Such a child had been born from the line of generations—a child whose lineage the one who best understood it could trace back to the ancestor of humanity, back to the young soul of humanity during the Lemurian Epoch, a child to whom he (St. Luke) could point as the reincarnated 'new Adam.' This child, whose soul was the mother-soul of humanity—a soul kept young through the ages—lived in such a way that all his youthful forces rayed into the astral body, and when the astral sheath was detached, it rose upwards and united with the Nirmanakaya of Buddha."

The Ancient Indian Triple "I Am"

1. Nirmāṇakāya, 'transformation body'—the manifestation of a Buddha in time and space. In Vajrayāna it is described as 'the dimension of ceaseless manifestation.'

2. Sambhogakāya, 'enjoyment-body,' 'rainbow body,' 'emanation body,'—this mind-made body is how Gautama Buddha and arhats are able to travel into heavenly realms using the continuum of the mind-stream. It also explains the miracles, emanating countless other bodies, projecting an infinite variety of forms in different realms simultaneously. Sambhogakaya-realms are known as Buddha-fields or Pure Lands.

3. Dharmakāya, 'dharma-body,' 'reality body,' 'inconceivable'—the Ātman (true self) of the Buddha present within all beings. It constitutes the unmanifested aspect of a buddha out of which buddhas arise and to which they return after their dissolution.

Buddha and Christianity

From Jesus to Christ, **Rudolf Steiner, Lecture VIII,** *The Two Jesus Children, Zoroaster and Buddha,* **Karlsruhe, October 12, 1911, GA 131**

"We know also that active in the astral body of this child were the forces which had once been acquired by that Bodhisattva who became Gautama Buddha. We know indeed—and in this respect the Oriental tradition is absolutely correct; for it can be confirmed by occult science—that the Bodhisattva, who on becoming Buddha five centuries before our era no longer needed to incarnate further on Earth, worked from the spiritual world upon all those who devoted themselves to his teachings. It is characteristic of such an individuality, who rises to heights from which he need no longer incarnate in a body of flesh, that he can then take part in the affairs and destiny of our Earth existence from out of the spiritual worlds. This can happen in the most manifold ways. In fact, the Bodhisattva who went through his last incarnation on the Earth as Gautama Buddha has taken an essential part in the further evolution of humanity. Our human spiritual world stands continually in connection with all the rest of the spiritual world. The human being not only eats and drinks and so takes into himself the substance of the physical Earth; he continually receives soul-spiritual nourishment from the spiritual world. In the most varied ways forces continually flow into physical earthly existence from out of the spiritual world. Such an in-flow of the forces which Buddha had gained for himself came into the wider stream of humanity through the fact that the Buddha forces permeated the astral body of the Nathan Jesus-child.

"Thus, we see the Buddha forces working further in the stream of Earth-existence which took its start from the Events of Palestine. For a long time, these Buddha forces have been working from the spiritual worlds, particularly upon everything in Western civilization which is unthinkable without the specific influence of Christianity. All those philosophical streams which have developed during recent centuries up to the nineteenth century, in so far as they are Western spiritual currents, are permeated by the Christ-Impulse; but the Buddha has always been working into them from out of the spiritual worlds. Hence the most important thing that European humanity can receive from Buddha today does not depend on the handing down of the teaching that Buddha gave to men about 500 years before the Christian era—*but on what he has become since that time.* For he has not remained at a standstill; he has progressed; and it is through this progress, as a spiritual being in the spiritual worlds, that he has in the highest sense been able to take part in the further evolution of Western civilization. For we know that the same individuality who appeared as Gautama Buddha in the East had previously worked in the West, and that certain legends and traditions connected with the name of Buddha or Wotan have to do with this same individuality, just as Buddhism has with Gautama Buddha in the East; hence the same field of action in human evolution which had been prepared earlier by the same individuality has again been occupied in a certain sense. Thus, are interlaced the ways taken by the spiritual currents within the evolution of humanity.

"Today the most important thing for us is to establish that in the astral body of the Jesus-child described by Luke we have the Buddha forces at work. And when this Nathan Jesus-child was twelve years old, the Zarathustra individuality passed over into his three-fold being."

The Gospel of St. Luke, Rudolf Steiner, Lecture III, *Buddhistic Conceptions in St. Luke,* Basel, September 17, 1909, GA 114

"Whoever turns to the *Gospel of St. Luke* will, to begin with, only be able to feel dimly something of what it contains; but an inkling will then dawn on him that whole worlds, vast spiritual worlds, are revealed by this *Gospel*. After what was said in the last lecture, this will be obvious to us; for as we heard, spiritual research shows how the Buddhistic world-conception, with everything it was able to give to mankind, flowed into the *Gospel of St. Luke*. It may truly be said that Buddhism radiates from this *Gospel*, but in a special form, comprehensible to the simplest and most unsophisticated mind.

"...Not only are the spiritual attainments of Buddhism presented to us through this *Gospel*; they come before us in an even nobler form, as though raised to a level higher than when they were a gift to humanity in India some six hundred years before our era.

"In the lecture yesterday, we spoke of Buddhism as the purest teaching of compassion and love; from the place in the world where

Buddha worked a gospel of love and compassion streamed into the whole spiritual evolution of the Earth. The gospel of love and compassion lives in the true Buddhist when his own heart feels the suffering confronting him in the outer world from all living creatures. There we encounter Buddhistic love and compassion in the fullest sense of the words; but from *The Gospel of St. Luke* there streams to us something that is more than this all-embracing love and compassion. It might be described as the translation of love and compassion into *deed*. Compassion in the highest sense of the word is the ideal of the Buddhist; the aim of one who lives according to the message of the *Gospel of St. Luke* is to unfold love that acts. The true Buddhist can himself share in the sufferings of the sick; from *The Gospel of St. Luke* comes the call to take active steps to do whatever is possible to bring about healing. Buddhism helps us to understand everything that stirs the human soul; *The Gospel of St. Luke* calls upon us to abstain from passing judgment, to do *more* than is done to us, to give *more* than we receive! Although in this *Gospel* there is the purest, most genuine Buddhism, love translated into *deed* must be regarded as a progression, a sublimation, of Buddhism…

"In the first place, it must be remembered that the Buddha had been a Bodhisattva, that is to say, a very lofty Being able to gaze deeply into the mysteries of existence. As a Bodhisattva, the Buddha had participated in the evolution of humanity throughout the ages. When in the Epoch following Atlantis the First Post-Atlantean Civilization was established and promoted, Buddha was already present as Bodhisattva and, acting as an intermediary, conveyed to man from the spiritual worlds the teachings indicated in the lecture yesterday. He had been present in Atlantean and even in Lemurian times. And because he had reached such a high stage of development, he was also able, during the twenty-nine years of his final existence as Bodhisattva, from his birth to the

moment when he became Buddha, to recollect stage-by-stage all
the communities in which he had lived before incarnating for the
last time in India…

"…At the age of twelve the astral sheath was cast off [of
Jesus] but did not dissolve in the universal astral world. Just
as it was, as the protective astral sheath of the young boy, with
all the vitalizing forces that had streamed into it between the
change of teeth and puberty, it now united with the Nirmanakaya
of Buddha. The spiritual body that had once appeared to the
shepherds as the radiant angelic host united with the astral
sheath released from the twelve-year-old Jesus, united with all
the forces through which the freshness of youth is maintained
during the period between the second dentition and puberty.
The Nirmanakaya which shone upon the Nathan Jesus-child
from birth onwards united with the astral sheath detached from
this child at puberty; it became one with this sheath and was
thereby rejuvenated. Through this rejuvenation, what Buddha had
formerly given to the world could be manifest again in the Jesus-
child. Hence the boy was able to speak with all the simplicity
of childhood about the lofty teachings of compassion and love
to which we have referred today. When Jesus was found in the
temple, he was speaking in a way that astonished those around
him, because he was enveloped by the Nirmanakaya of Buddha,
refreshed as from a fountain of youth by the boy's astral sheath."

The Gospel of St. Luke, Rudolf Steiner, Lecture IX, *Buddha's Teaching of Compassion and Love,* September 25, 1909, GA 114

"We have heard that Buddha brought to mankind the great
teaching of compassion and love. Here is one of the instances
where what is said in occultism must be taken exactly as it
stands, for otherwise it might be objected that at one time Christ

is said to have brought love to the Earth, and at another that Buddha brought the teaching of love. But is that the same? On one occasion I said that Buddha brought the *teaching* of love to the Earth and on another occasion that Christ brought love itself as a *living power* to the Earth. That is the great difference. Close attention is necessary when the deepest concerns of humanity are being considered; for otherwise what happens is that information given in one place is presented somewhere else in a quite different form and then it is said that in order to be fair to everybody I have proclaimed two messengers of love! The very closest attention is essential in occultism. When this enables us really to understand the words in which the momentous truths are clothed, they are seen in the right light.

"Knowing that the great teaching of compassion and love brought by Buddha is given expression in the Eightfold Path, we may ask ourselves: What is the aim of this Eightfold Path? What does a man attain when from the depths of his soul he adopts it as his life's ideal, never losing sight of the goal and asking continually: How can I reach the greatest perfection? How can I purify my Ego most completely? What must I do to enable my Ego to fulfil its function in the world as perfectly as possible?— Such a man will say to himself: If I obey every precept of the Eightfold Path my Ego will reach the greatest perfection that it is possible to conceive. Everything is a matter of the purification and ennoblement of the Ego; everything that can stream from this wonderful Eightfold Path must penetrate into us. The point of importance is that it is work carried out by the Ego, for its own perfecting. If, therefore, men were to develop to further stages in themselves that which Buddha set in motion as the 'Wheel of the Law' (that is the technical term), their Egos would gradually become possessed of wisdom at a high level—wisdom in the form of *thought*—and they would recognize the signs of perfection. Buddha brought to humanity the wisdom of love and compassion, and when we succeed in making the whole astral body a product of the Eightfold Path, we shall possess the requisite knowledge of the laws expressed in its teachings.

"But there is a difference between wisdom in the form of *thought* and wisdom as *living power*; there is a difference between knowing what the Ego must become and allowing the living power to flow into our very being so that it may stream forth again from the Ego into all the world as it streamed from Christ, working upon the astral, etheric and physical bodies of those around Him. The impulse given by the great Buddha enabled humanity to have knowledge of the teaching of compassion and love. What Christ brought is first and foremost a *living power*, not a teaching. He sacrificed His very Self, He descended in order to flow not merely into the astral bodies of men but into the Ego, so that the Ego itself should have the power to ray out love as *substantiality*. Christ brought to the Earth the substantiality, the living essence of love, not merely the wisdom-filled content of love. That is the all-important point.

"Nineteen centuries and roughly five more have now elapsed since the great Buddha lived on the Earth; in about three thousand years from now—this we learn from occultism—a considerable number of human beings will have reached the stage of being able to evolve the wisdom of the Buddha, the Eightfold Path, out of their own moral nature, out of their own heart and soul. Buddha had once to be on Earth, and the power that mankind will develop little-by-little as the wisdom of the Eightfold Path proceeded from him; after about three thousand years from now men will be able to unfold its teaching from within themselves; it will then be their own possession and they will no longer be obliged to receive it from outside. Then they will be able to say: *This Eightfold Path springs from our very selves as the wisdom of compassion and love.*

"Even if nothing else had happened than the setting in motion of the Wheel of the Law by the great Buddha, in three thousand years from now humanity would have become capable of knowing the doctrine of compassion and love. But it is a different matter also to have acquired the faculty to embody it in very life. Not only to know about compassion and love, but under the influence of an Individuality to unfold it as *living power*—there lies the difference. This faculty proceeded from Christ. He poured love itself into men and it will grow from strength to strength. When men have reached the end of their evolution, wisdom will have revealed to them the content of the doctrine of compassion and love—*this they will owe to Buddha*. But at the same time they will possess the faculty of letting the love stream out from the Ego over mankind—*this they will owe to Christ*."

The Reappearance of Christ in the Etheric, Rudolf Steiner, Lecture III, *Buddhism and Pauline Christianity*, Köln, February 27, 1910, GA 118

"There is a great distinction between the spiritual stream that came from Buddha and the one that arose from the Christ impulse. This is not meant to place these streams in opposition to one another; it is rather necessary to understand in what regard each of these streams can be fruitful. Both streams must unite in the future, and Christianity must be fructified by spiritual science. For a time, Christianity had to set aside the teaching of reincarnation. It was included in the esoteric teaching; but could not be received in exoteric Christianity for certain universal pedagogical reasons. In contrast, reincarnation was a fundamental principle of Buddhism. There it was bound up with the teaching of suffering—which is exactly what Christianity is intended to overcome. Once we have recognized the purposes and missions of both streams, we will also be able to distinguish clearly between them. The main distinction can be seen most strongly when one examines the two individualities, Buddha and Paul.

"Gautama Buddha came to knowledge through his enlightenment under the Bodhi tree; he then taught that this world is maya. It cannot be considered real—because therein lies maya, the great illusion that one believes it to be real. Man must strive to be released from the realm of the elements; then he comes into a realm, Nirvāṇa, where neither names nor things exist. Only then is man freed from illusion. The realm of maya is suffering. Birth, death, sickness, and age are suffering. It is the thirst for existence that brings man into this realm. Once he has freed himself from this thirst, he no longer needs to incarnate. One can ask oneself why the great Buddha preached this doctrine. The answer can follow only from a consideration of the evolutionary course of humanity.

"Man was not always the way he is today. In earlier times, man not only had his physical body at his disposal for achieving knowledge, but there was also a kind of clairvoyant knowledge diffused among human beings. Man knew that there were spiritual hierarchies in the same way that we know that there are plants. He had no power of judgment but could see the creative beings themselves. This wisdom gradually disappeared, but a memory of it remained. In ancient India, Persia, even in Egypt, there was still a memory of previous earthly lives. The human soul at that time was such that one knew:— *'I was descended from divine beings, but my incarnations have gradually penetrated the physical so strongly that my spiritual gaze has been darkened.'*

"Man experienced the progress in this time as a degeneration, as a step backward. This was felt especially by all those who could still, even in much later times, leave their physical bodies at particular moments. The everyday world appeared to them in these moments as a world of illusion, as maya, the great deception. Buddha only spoke out of what lived in the human soul. The physical, sensible world was experienced as that which had pulled man down; he wished to leave this world and ascend again. The world of the senses bore the guilt for the descent of humanity.

"Let us compare this conception with the Christ impulse and the teachings of Paul. Paul did not call the sensible world an illusion, although he knew as well as Buddha that man had descended from the spiritual worlds and that it was his urge for existence that had brought him into this world. One speaks in a Christian sense, however, when one asks if this urge for existence is always something bad. Is the physical, sensible world only deception? According to Paul's conception, it is not the urge for existence in itself that is evil; this urge was originally good—*but became harmful through the fall of man, under the influence of Luciferic beings*. This urge was not always harmful; but it has become so and has brought sickness, lies, suffering, and so on. What was a cosmic event in Buddha's conception became a human event for Paul.

"Had the Luciferic influence not interfered, man would have seen the truth in the physical world rather than illusion. It is not the world of the senses that is wrong but human knowledge that has been dulled through the Luciferic influence. The differences in these conceptions bring different conclusions with them. Buddha sought redemption in a world in which nothing of this world of the senses remained. Paul said that man should

purify his forces, his thirst for existence, because he himself
had corrupted them. Man should tear away the veil that covers
the truth and, through purifying himself, see again the truth he
himself had covered. In place of the veil that conceals the plant
world, for example, he will see the divine-spiritual forces that
work on and behind the plants. Rend the veil, and the world of
the senses becomes transparent—*we finally see the realm of the
spirit.* We believed we saw the animal, the plant, and the mineral
kingdoms; that was our error. In reality—*we saw the hierarchies
streaming toward us.*

"That is why Paul said:— *'Kill not the pleasure of existence;
rather purify it, because it was originally good.'* This can occur
when man takes the power of Christ into himself. When this
power has permeated the soul, it drives away the soul's darkness.
The gods did not place man on the Earth for no purpose. It is
man's duty to overcome what hinders him from seeing this world
spiritually. Buddha's conclusion that one must shun incarnation
points to an archetypal wisdom for humanity. Paul, in contrast,
said:— *'Go through incarnation, but imbue yourselves with Christ,
and in a distant future all that man has cast up as illusion will
vanish.'* This teaching, which put the blame not on the physical,
sensible world—*but on man himself,* had of necessity to become
a historic doctrine. Exactly for this reason, however, it could not
be given in its entirety at the beginning. Only the initial impulse
could be given, which must be penetrated. This impulse would
then gradually enter all spheres of life. Although almost two
thousand years have passed since the Mystery of Golgotha, the
Christ impulse is only beginning today to be received. Whole
spheres of life, such as philosophy and science, have yet to be
imbued with it. Buddha was more able to give his teaching all
at once because he referred to an ancient wisdom that was still

experienced in his time. The Christ impulse, however, must prevail gradually. A theory of knowledge based on these facts contrasts sharply with that of Kant, who did not know that it is our knowledge itself that must be purified.

"Paul had to instruct human beings that the work in each individual incarnation is actually of great importance. In contrast to the relatively recent doctrine of the Buddha that the individual incarnation is worthless, he almost had to overstate this teaching. One must learn to declare:—

'Not I, but Christ in me!'

This is the purified I. Through Paul, spiritual life became dependent upon this one incarnation for all the future. Now that such an education of the soul has been completed and a sufficient number of human beings have gone through it in the past two thousand years, the time has come again to teach reincarnation and karma. We must seek to restore our I to the condition in which it was before incarnations began.

"It is always said that Christ is constantly in our midst. *"I am with you every day until the end of the Earth."* Now, however, man must learn to behold Christ and to believe that what he sees is real. This will happen in the near future, already in this century, and in the following two thousand years more and more people will experience it…

"…Even in this century, and increasingly throughout the next 2,500 years, human beings will become able to behold Christ in His etheric form. They will behold the etheric Earth from which the plant world springs up. They will also be able to see, however, that inner goodness works differently on the environment from evil. He who possesses this science in the highest degree is the

Maitreya Buddha, who will come in approximately 3,000 years. 'Maitreya Buddha' means the 'Buddha of right-mindedness.' He is the one who will make clear for human beings the significance of right-mindedness. This will all lead human beings to know in which direction they must go. You must undertake to transform abstract ideals into concrete ideals in order to contribute to an evolution that moves forward. If we do not succeed in this, the Earth will sink into materialism, and humanity will have to begin again, either on the Earth, after a great catastrophe, or on the next planet. The Earth needs anthroposophy! Whoever realizes this is an anthroposophist."

The Spiritual Hierarchies, Rudolf Steiner, Lecture VII, *Dhyani-Buddha, Bodhisattva, Buddha,* Düsseldorf, April 16, 1909, GA 110

"In the Post-Atlantean times men had not yet advanced so far that they could do without help from above, inspiration was still necessary; and a sort of ensouling still took place from above. We have seen how such ensouling occurred in Lemurian times, because a Spirit of Personality [Archai] ensouled the physical body; in the Atlantean times the physical and the etheric bodies were ensouled by Archangels, and now the great leaders of the Post-Atlantean times were ensouled through an Angel descending into their physical, etheric and astral bodies. The great leaders of humanity in the Post-Atlantean times did not possess merely a physical, etheric and astral body—*but an Angel also lived within them.* Therefore, these great leaders could look back into their former incarnations. The ordinary man cannot do so as yet, because he has not yet developed his Manas [Spirit-Self]; he must himself first become an Angel. These leaders, who were born out of the ordinary inhabitants, carried an Angelic

Being within their physical, etheric and astral bodies, who ensouled and interpenetrated them. This is again Maya, again we have Beings who are something different from what they appear to be on Earth. The great leaders of humanity of grey antiquity were quite different from what they outwardly seemed to be. They were personalities in whom an Angel dwelt and gave what they needed, so that they might become Teachers and Leaders of men. The great founders of religions were men possessed by Angels. Angels spoke through them. The affairs of the world have to be described indeed as entirely regular—but the processes of development always interpenetrate one within the other, they overlap. That which we describe as exhibiting complete regularity does not work itself out with such regularity. It is certainly true that, as a general principle, Spirits of Personality did speak through human entities in the Lemurian times, Archangels in the Atlantean, and Angels in the Post-Atlantean times. But such beings arose, also even in the Post-Atlantean times, who were penetrated by a Spirit of Personality down to their physical body, who, therefore, were in the same position, although they lived in the Post-Atlantean times, as were those beings through whom in Lemuria the Spirits of Personality spoke. Thus, it was possible to have men also in the Post-Atlantean times, who bore externally all the characteristics of their nation; but who, because humanity still needed such great leaders, carried within them a Spirit of Personality—and who were the external incarnation of such a Spirit. Then there were also men in the Post-Atlantean times who had an Archangel, a Spirit of Mercury, within them, who ensouled their physical and etheric bodies. And lastly, a third category of men was ensouled, inspired in their physical, etheric, and astral bodies by an Angel Being, one through whom an Angel spoke. In the spirit of the Eastern Teachings, such personalities received particular names. Thus, a personality who outwardly resembles a man of our Post-Atlantean times; but who really is the bearer of a Spirit of Personality, who is ensouled by that Spirit down to his physical body, is called Dhyani-Buddha in the Eastern Teachings. Dhyani-Buddha is a generic name for human individualities in whom the Spirits of Personality are active, even as far as their physical body.

"Those personalities who are ensouled down to their etheric body, who were bearers of Archangels in the Post-Atlantean times, are called Bodhisattva and those who are the bearers of an Angel, who are, therefore, ensouled in their physical, etheric, and astral bodies, are called human Buddhas.

"Thus, we have three degrees: that of the Dhyani-Buddha, the Bodhisattva, and the human Buddha. This is the true teaching of the Buddhas, of the classes and categories of Buddhas which we have to recognize in connection with the whole manner and means by which the Hierarchies fulfil their ends. This is the marvel which meets us, when we look back to earlier undeveloped men, that among these men we find those, through whom the Hierarchies speak. The great Hierarchies speak out of the Cosmos downwards into the Planets, and only by degrees do these Spirits of the higher Hierarchies, who were active before the appearance of our Earth, emancipate the planetary men who live down here, when they have reached the necessary degree of ripeness. Here we gaze into unfathomable depths of wisdom. And what is of extraordinary importance is, that we understand this wisdom exactly as it was taught in all the ages, when primeval wisdom was taught to men.

"Thus, when you hear of the Buddhas, for they do not speak of the one Buddha only in the Eastern teaching, but of many, among whom there are naturally different grades of perfection—give attention to the fact: a Buddha walks on Earth, but behind the Buddha, was the Bodhisattva and even the Dhyani-Buddha.

"Matters, however, might be so, that the Dhyani-Buddha or the Bodhisattva did not reach so far as to ensoul the physical body; but that the Bodhisattva descended only as far as to be able to ensoul the etheric body, so that you can imagine a Being who does not reach so far as to ensoul and inspire the man's physical body, but only the etheric body. It can, however, happen when such a Bodhisattva is not physically visible (for when he appears only in an etheric body, he is not physically visible, and there were such Bodhisattva who were physically invisible) that he can, as a higher Being, inspire quite exceptionally the human Buddha. So that we have the human Buddha, who is already inspired by an Angelic Being, being further inspired in his etheric body by an Archangel Being. It is essential that we should look into this wonderful complexity of human nature. Many Individualities to whom we look back into former times can only be understood, when we accept them as the meeting point of different higher Beings, who proclaim and express themselves through the man. Sometimes one single personality has to be ensouled by different individualities of the higher Hierarchies. And sometimes it is not only the inhabitants of Mercury who speak with us, when we have a certain personality standing before us, but the inhabitants of Venus also…

Editorial Notes:—

1. A Spirit of Personality [Archai] enters the Physical and the entity is called a Dyani-Buddha in Post-Atlantean times.
2. An Archangel enters the Physical and Etheric and the entity is called a Bodhisattva in Post-Atlantean times.

3. An Angel enters the Physical, Etheric and Astral and the entity is
    called a human Buddha in Post-Atlantean times."

Turning Points Spiritual History, **Rudolf Steiner, Lecture III,**
Buddha -or- Buddhism and Christianity, **Berlin, March 2, 1911,**
GA 60

"In these days there is much discussion concerning 'The Buddha
and the Buddhist Creed'; and this fact is the more interesting
to all who follow the course of human evolution, because
a knowledge of the true character of the Buddhist religion,
or perhaps more correctly, the longing felt by many for its
comprehension has only recently entered into the spiritual life of
the Western nations...

"It is a remarkable fact that most people still persist in
associating Buddhism, primarily, with the idea of recurrent
Earth lives, to which concept we have often referred in
these lectures. Such an assumption is, however, found to be
unwarranted when we have regard to the essential character
of the Buddhist belief. Hence, we must regard as the essential
moving principle underlying the whole trend of Buddhist
spiritual thought that principle which operates in the direction of
freedom, that is, redemption from repeated rebirth, or liberation
from reincarnation which it accepts as an established and
unquestionable fact; in this concept is expressed the true and vital
essence of Buddhism.

"Even from a superficial glance at the history of Western
spiritual life, we learn that the idea of repeated earthly existence
is quite independent of an understanding of Buddhism, and
vice versa; for during the course of our Occidental spiritual
development we find ourselves confronted with a conception of
reincarnation, presented in a manner both lofty and sublime,

by a personality who most certainly had remained untouched by Buddhist views and trend of thought. This personality was Lessing, who in his treatise on *The Education of Mankind*, which is regarded as the most mature and mellow of his works, closes with the confession that he himself was a believer in the Doctrine of Reincarnation…

"I have persistently endeavored to make it clear that the idea of reincarnation, both with regard to Spiritual Science and Theosophy, was not derived from any one of the ancient traditions, not even from Buddhism; it has in fact thrust itself upon us during our time, as a result of independent observation and reflection concerning life in connection with spiritual investigation…

"Indian thought ever harked back to that dim past when man was truly united with the Spirit-World. For there came a time when the Indian fell away from his exalted spiritual standard; this decline persisted until a certain level was reached, when he rose again, only to sink once more. He continued to alternate in this fashion throughout the ages, every descent taking him still further along the downward path, while each upward step was, as it were, a mitigation granted by some higher power, in order that man might not be compelled to work and live, all too suddenly, in that condition which he had already entered upon during his *fall*. According to ancient Indian philosophy, as each period of decline was ended, there arose a certain outstanding figure whose personality was known as a 'Buddha'; the last of these was incarnated as the son of King Suddhodana and called Gautama Buddha.

"Since those olden times, when humanity was still directly united with the Spirit-World, there have arisen a number of such Buddhas, five having appeared subsequent to the last fall. The advent of the Buddhas was a sign that mankind shall not sink into illusion—into Maya—but that again and again there shall come into men's lives something of the ancient primal wisdom, to succor and to aid humanity. This primordial knowledge, however, because of man's constant downward trend, fades from time-to-time; but in order that it shall be renewed there arises periodically a new Buddha, and as we have stated, the last of these was Gautama Buddha.

"Before such great teachers could advance, through repeated Earth lives, to the dignity of Buddhahood, if we may so express it, they must have already been exalted and attained the lofty standing of a Bodhisattva. According to the Indian philosophical outlook, Gautama Buddha, up to his twenty-ninth year, was not regarded as a Buddha, but as a Bodhisattva. It was therefore as a Bodhisattva that he was born into the royal house of Suddhodana; and because his life was ever devoted to toil and to striving, he was at last blessed with that inner illumination, symbolically portrayed in the words, 'Sitting under the Bodhi tree'; and that glorious enlightenment which flowed in upon him found expression in the 'Sermon at Benares.'

"Thus did Gautama Buddha rise to the full dignity of Buddhahood in his twenty-ninth year, and from that time on, he was empowered to revive once again a last remnant of by-gone primeval wisdom, which however, in the light of Indian conceptions, would be destined to fall into decadence during the centuries to come. But according to these same concepts, when man has sunk so low, that the wisdom and the knowledge which this last Buddha brought, shall have waned, then will yet another Bodhisattva rise to Buddhahood, the Buddha of the Future—the Maitreya Buddha; who's coming the Indian surely awaits, for it is foretold in his philosophy…

"Thus, it was the Buddha realized from the moment of his illumination that in the teachings and experience born of affliction, lay that basic element necessary to humanity for its future progress; and he conceived a factor (wherein was no wisdom) which he termed *The Thirst for Existence* to be the true source of all that misery and sorrow which so troubles the world. Upon the one side wisdom, upon the other a thirst for existence, where wisdom has no part. It was this thought which caused Gautama to exclaim:—

'Only liberation from recurrent Earth life can lead humanity to the realization of perfect freedom; for earthly wisdom, even that of the highest learning, cannot save us from grief and anguish.'

He therefore gave himself up to meditation, and sought some means whereby mankind might be led away from all this restlessness in the world of his reincarnations, and guided into that transcendent state which Gautama Buddha has designated Nirvāṇa"

"What then, is the nature of this state—this World of Nirvāṇa—which man shall enter when he has so advanced in his earthly life that 'The Thirst for Existence' has passed, and he no more desires to be reborn? Nirvāṇa is a condition that can only be characterized in the Buddhist sense. According to this conception, it is a world of redemption and of bliss that can never be expressed in terms of things which may be apprehended in the material state in which we have our being. There is nothing in this physical world, nor in the wide expanse of the cosmos, which can awaken in mankind a realization of the sublime truth underlying such redemption…

"The innermost essence of Buddhism is best understood by
comparing the Buddhist creed with that of Christianity. When
we do this, we at once realize why it was that Lessing should
have made use of the phrase,—'Is not all Eternity mine?'—in
his book entitled *The Education of Mankind*. These words imply
that if we employ the experiences gained during our repeated
reincarnations, in such manner as to suffer the Christ-force to
abide ever more and more within us, we shall at last reach the
eternal spheres which realms we cannot as yet hope to attain,
because we have of our own act, enveloped the inner being
as with a veil. The idea of reincarnation will present a wholly
different aspect when illumined by the glory of Christianity;
but it is not merely the actual belief in rebirth which matters for
the present, for with the advance of Christian culture, humanity
will gradually be driven to the acceptance of this concept as a
truth brought forward by Spiritual Science. But it is important
that we should realize that, whereas the deepest sentiments and
convictions of the Buddhist's faith cause him to blame the World
for everything that is Maya—the Christian, on the other hand,
looks upon himself, and mankind in general, as responsible for
all earthly deception and illusion. The while he stores within
his innermost being those qualities which are prerequisite and
necessary to him, in order that he may rise to that state which we
term Redemption. In the Christian sense, however, this does not
only imply deliverance, but actual resurrection; for when man has
attained to this state, his Ego is already raised to the level of that
more exalted 'I' from which he has fallen. The Buddhist, when
he looks around upon the world, finds himself concerned with
an original sin, but feels that he has been placed upon this Earth
merely for a time, he therefore desires his freedom. The Christian
likewise realizes his connection with an original sin but seeks

amendment and to atone for this first transgression. Such is an historical line of thought, for while the Christian feels that his present existence is associated with an incident which took place in olden times among the ancients, he also connects his life with an event that will surely come to pass when he is so advanced that his whole being will shine forth, filled with that radiance which we designate as the essence of the Christ-Being.

"Hence it is that during the world's development we find nothing in Christianity corresponding to successive Buddha-epochs coming one after another, as one might say, un-historically, each Buddha proclaiming a like doctrine. Christianity brings forward but one single glorious event during the whole of man's earthly progress. In the same way as the Buddhist pictures the Buddha, seated isolated and alone under the Bodhi tree, at the moment when he was exalted, and the great illumination came to him; so, does the Christian visualize Jesus of Nazareth at that time when there descended upon Him the all-inspiring *Spirit of the Cosmos*. The baptism of Christ by John, as described in the *Bible*, is as vivid and clear a picture as is the Buddhist's conception of the Illumination of the Buddha. Thus, we have in the first case, the Buddha seated under the Bodhi tree, concerned only with his own soul; in the second, Jesus of Nazareth, standing in the Jordan, while there descended upon Him that cosmic essence, that Spirit, symbolically represented as a dove, which entered into His innermost being."

Buddha and Christ: The Sphere of the Bodhisattvas, Rudolf Steiner, Milan, September 21, 1911, GA 130

"The powers and forces which draw man upwards again to the spiritual world fall into two categories: those which draw him upwards on the path of Wisdom, and those which draw him upwards on the path of Morality. The forces to which intellectual progress is mainly due all proceed from the impulse given by a great Individuality of the Fourth Post-Atlantean Period who is known to you all, namely Gautama Buddha. It is a remarkable discovery of spiritual investigation that the most penetrating, most significant, thoughts conceived in our present Period have proceeded from Gautama Buddha. This is all the more remarkable inasmuch as until the days of Schopenhauer [German philosopher, Feb. 22, 1788–Sep. 21, 1860]—therefore by no means long ago—the name of Gautama Buddha was almost unknown in the West...

"...Consciousness of this truth was demonstrated in a beautiful legend written down by John of Damascus in the eighth century and well known throughout Europe in the Middle Ages. It is the legend of Barlaam and Joshaphat, which relates how he who had become the successor of Buddha (Joshaphat is a phonetic variation of 'Bodhisattva') received teaching from Barlaam about the Christ-impulse. The legend, which was subsequently forgotten, tells us that the Bodhisattva who succeeded Gautama Buddha was instructed by Barlaam and his soul was fired by the Christian-impulse. This was the second impulse which, in addition to that of Buddha, continues to work in the evolution of humanity. It is the Christ-impulse and is connected with the future ascent of humanity to Morality. Although Buddha's teaching is in a particular sense moral teaching, the Christ-impulse is not teaching but actual power which works as such and to an increasing degree imbues mankind with moral strength. (I *Corinthians* IV:20) ...

"Before the Event of Golgotha, the Bodhisattva, who was the successor of Buddha, was present on the Earth in order to prepare for that event and give teaching to those around him.

He incarnated in the personality of Jeshu ben Pandira one century before the birth of Jesus of Nazareth. Thus, we must distinguish between the Jeshu ben Pandira-incarnation of the Bodhisattva who was the successor of Gautama Buddha, and the incarnation at the beginning of our Era of Jesus of Nazareth who for three years of his life was permeated by the cosmic Being we call the Christ.

"The Bodhisattva who incarnated in Jeshu ben Pandira and in other personalities too, returns again and again, until in about three thousand years from now, he will attain Buddha-hood and as Maitreya Buddha live through his final incarnation. The Christ-individuality was on the Earth in the body of Jesus of Nazareth for three years only and *does not come again in a physical body*; in the Fifth Post-Atlantean Period [1,414 A.D.-3,574 A.D.] He comes in an etheric body, in the Sixth Period [3,574 A.D.-5,734 A.D.] in an astral body, and in the Seventh [5,734 A.D.-7,894 A.D.] in a mighty Cosmic Ego that is like a great Group-Soul of humanity."

"When a human being dies, his physical, etheric and astral bodies fall away from him and his ego passes over to the next incarnation. It is exactly the same with the planet Earth. What is physical in our Earth falls away at the end of the Earth-period and human souls in their totality pass over into the Jupiter condition, the next planetary embodiment of the Earth. And just as in the case of an individual human being the ego is the center of his further evolution, so for the whole of future humanity the Christ-Ego in the astral and etheric bodies of men goes on to ensoul the Jupiter-existence. We therefore see how starting from a physical man on Earth—the *Christ gradually evolves as Etheric Christ, as Astral Christ, as Ego-Christ, in order, as Ego-Christ, to be the Spirit of the Earth who then rises to even higher stages together with all mankind.*

"What are we doing when we teach Spiritual Science today? We are teaching what Oriental wisdom so clearly proclaimed when the Bodhisattva who was then the son of King Suddhodana, attained Buddha-hood. In those Oriental teachings was expressed the realization that it was the task of the next Bodhisattva—who would eventually become a Buddha—to spread over the Earth the knowledge that would reveal Christ to men in the true light. Thus, the Bodhisattva, who incarnated in Jeshu ben Pandira and again and again in others, became the great Teacher of the Christ Impulse. This is indicated very clearly in the legend of Barlaam and Joshaphat, which tells how Joshaphat (i.e. the Bodhisattva) is instructed by Barlaam, the Christian teacher. The Oriental occult teachings call this Bodhisattva the 'Bringer of the Good'—Maitreya Buddha. And we know from occult investigations that in this Maitreya Buddha the power of the Word will be present in a degree of which men of the present time can, as yet, have no conception. It is possible today through higher clairvoyant perception of the process of world-evolution to discover how the Maitreya Buddha will teach after three thousand years have passed. Much of his teaching can also be expressed in symbolic forms. But today—because mankind is insufficiently mature—it is not yet possible to utter words such as those that will come from the lips of the Maitreya Buddha."

"In the Eightfold Path, Gautama Buddha gave the great intellectual teachings of right speech, right thinking, right action, and so on. The words uttered by the Maitreya Buddha will contain a magic power that will become moral impulses in the men who hear them. And if there should be a gospel telling of the Maitreya Buddha, the writer of it would have to use words differing from those used of Christ in the *Gospel of St. John*:—

'And the Word was made Flesh.'

The evangelist of the Maitreya Buddha would have to testify:—

'And the Flesh was made *Word*.'

The utterances of the Maitreya Buddha will be permeated in a miraculous way with the power of Christ."

Buddha and the Maitreya Buddha

The utterances of the Maitreya Buddha will be permeated in a miraculous way with the power of Christ. Spiritual Scientific investigations show us that, in a certain respect, even the external life of the Maitreya Buddha will be patterned on the life of Christ. What happens is that when this human being has reached a certain age, his ego is taken out of his bodily sheaths and a different ego passes into his body. The greatest example of this is Christ Jesus Himself, of whom in his thirtieth year the Christ-individuality had taken possession. All the incarnations of the Bodhisattva who will become the Maitreya Buddha have shown that in this sense, his life will resemble that of Christ.

In none of the incarnations of the Bodhisattva is it known, either in his childhood or youth, that he will become a Bodhisattva. Whenever the Bodhisattva becomes Buddha there is evidence that at the age of 30 or 31, another individuality takes possession of his body. The Bodhisattva will never reveal himself as such in his early youth; but in his thirtieth or thirty-first year he will manifest quite different qualities, because another Being takes possession of his body.

In our period of evolution, two streams of spiritual life are at work; one of them is the stream of Wisdom, or the Buddha-stream, containing the most sublime teaching of wisdom, goodness of heart, and peace on Earth. To enable this teaching of Buddha to permeate the hearts of all mankind, *the Christ-impulse is indispensable*. The second stream is the Christ-stream itself which will lead humanity from intellectuality, by way of aesthetic feeling and insight, to morality.

And the greatest teacher of the Christ-impulse, in all ages, will be the successor of that Bodhisattva who incarnates again and again and who, in three thousand years from now, will become the Maitreya Buddha. For the statement contained in Oriental chronicles is true: that exactly five thousand years after Gautama Buddha attained Enlightenment under the Bodhi tree, the Maitreya Buddha will incarnate on Earth for the last time.

The succession of Bodhisattvas and Buddhas has no relation as such to the cosmic Being we call Christ; it was a Bodhisattva—not the Christ—who incarnated in the body of Jeshu ben Pandira. Christ incarnated in a physical body once, and only once, for a period of three years. The Bodhisattva appears in every century until his incarnation as Maitreya Buddha.

The mission of Anthroposophy today is to be a synthesis of religion, philosophy and science. We can conceive of one form of religion being comprised in Buddhism, another form in Christianity, and as evolution proceeds the more closely do the different religions unite—in the way that Buddha and Christ themselves are united.

The Being of Elijah and the Astral Body of Buddha

The Gospel of St. Luke, Rudolf Steiner, Lecture VI, *The Mission of the Hebrews,* Basel, September 20, 1909, GA 114

"When this Individuality was born again, he was to unite with the body of the child born to Zacharias and Elisabeth. We know from the *Gospel* itself that John the Baptist is to be regarded as the reborn Elijah. But in him we have to do with an Individuality who in his earlier incarnations had not habitually developed or brought fully into operation all the forces present in the normal course of life. In the normal course of life, the inner power or force of the Ego becomes active while the physical body of the human being is developing in the mother's womb. The Elijah-Individuality in earlier times had not descended deeply enough to be involved in the inner processes operating here. The Ego had not, as in normal circumstances, been stirred into activity by its own forces, but from outside. This was now to happen again. But the Ego was now farther from the spiritual world and nearer to the Earth, much more closely connected with the Earth than the Beings who had formerly guided Elijah. The transition leading to the amalgamation of the Buddha-stream with the Zarathustra-stream was now to be brought about.

"Everything was to be rejuvenated. It was now the Buddha who had to work from outside—the Being who had linked himself with the Earth and its affairs and now, in his Nirmanakaya [Astral form], was united with the Nathan Jesus. This Being who on the one side was united with the Earth but on the other withdrawn from it because he was working only in his Nirmanakaya which had soared to realms 'beyond' the Earth and hovered above the head of the Nathan Jesus—this Being had now to work from outside and stimulate the Ego-force of John the Baptist.

"Thus, it was the Nirmanakaya of Buddha which now stirred the Ego-force of John into activity, having the same effect as spiritual forces that had formerly worked upon Elijah. At certain times the being known as Elijah had been rapt in states of ecstasy; then the God spoke, filling his Ego with a force which could be communicated to the outer world. Now again a spiritual force was present—the Nirmanakaya of Buddha hovering above the head of the Nathan Jesus; this force worked upon Elisabeth when John was to be born, stimulated within her the embryo of John in the sixth month of pregnancy, and wakened the Ego. But being nearer to the Earth this force now worked as more than an inspiration;

it had an actual formative effect upon the Ego of John. Under the influence of the visit of her who is there called 'Mary,' the Ego of John the Baptist awoke into activity. The Nirmanakaya of Buddha was here working upon the Ego of the former Elijah—now the Ego of John the Baptist—wakening it and penetrating right into the physical substance.

"What may we now expect?

"Even as the words of power once spoken by Elijah in the ninth century before our era were in truth 'God's words', and the actions performed by his hands 'God's actions', it was now to be the same in the case of John the Baptist, inasmuch as what had been present in Elijah had come to life again. The Nirmanakaya of Buddha worked as an inspiration into the Ego of John the Baptist. That which manifested itself to the shepherds and hovered above the head of the Nathan Jesus extended its power into John the Baptist, whose preaching was primarily the re-awakened preaching of Buddha. This fact is in the highest degree noteworthy and cannot fail to make a deep impression upon us when we recall the sermon at Benares wherein Buddha spoke of the suffering in life and the release from it through the Eightfold Path. He often expanded a sermon by saying in effect: 'Hitherto you have had the teaching of the Brahmans; they ascribe their origin to Brahma himself and claim to be superior to other men because of this noble descent. These Brahmans claim that a man's worth is determined by his descent, but I say to you: Man's worth is determined by what he makes of himself, *not* by what is in him by virtue of his descent. Judged by the great wisdom of the world, man's worth lies in whatever he makes of himself as an individual!'—Buddha aroused the wrath of the Brahmans because he emphasized the individual quality in men, saying:—

'Verily it is of no avail to call yourselves Brahmans; what matters is that each one of you, through his own personal qualities and efforts should make of himself a purified individual.'

Although not word for word, such was the gist of many of Buddha's sermons. And he would often expand this teaching by showing how, when a man understands the world of suffering, he can feel compassion, can become a comforter and a helper, how he shares the lot of others because he knows that he is feeling the same suffering and the same pain...

"Knowing that these Beings appear on the physical plane at different turning-points of time, we learn to understand the unity of religions and the spiritual proclamations made to mankind. We shall not realize who and what Buddha was by clinging to tradition but by listening to how he actually speaks. Five to six hundred years before our era, Buddha preached the Sermon at Benares, but his voice has not been silenced. He speaks, although no longer incarnated, when he inspires through the Nirmanakaya. *From the mouth of John the Baptist we hear what the Buddha had to say six hundred years after he had lived in a physical body.*"

Black Sea School of Skythianos

The Spiritual Foundation of Morality, **Rudolf Steiner, Lecture II, Norrköping, May 29, 1912, GA 155**

"People, who to begin with had external teachers in the physical world, came together there [at the Mystery Center established by Skythianos on the East coast of the Black Sea]. They were instructed in the doctrines and principles which had proceeded from Buddhism; but these were permeated by the impulses which came into the world through Christianity. Then, after the pupils had been sufficiently prepared, they were brought to where the deeper forces lying within them, the deeper forces of wisdom could be brought forth, so that they were led to clairvoyant vision of the spiritual world and were able to see into the spiritual worlds. The first thing attained by the pupils of this occult school, was, for example, the recognition of those who no longer descended to the physical plane. But this they could only do after they had been accustomed to it by the teachers incarnated in the physical body. In this way they came to know Buddha. Thus, these occult pupils learned to know Buddha face to face if one may so speak of his spiritual being. In this way he continued to work spiritually in the occult pupils and thus his power worked down to the physical plane, although he himself no longer descended to physical embodiment in the physical world.

"Now the pupils in this occult school were grouped according to their maturity into two unequal divisions, and only the more advanced were chosen for the smaller division. Most of these pupils were able to become so clairvoyant that they came in touch with a being who strove with all his might to bring his impulses through to the physical world, and although he himself did not descend into this world they learned all the secrets of Buddha and all that he wished to have accomplished. Most of these pupils remained as such—clairvoyants; but there were some who, in addition to the qualities of knowledge and of psychic clairvoyance, had developed the spiritual element to a remarkable degree, which cannot be separated from a certain humility, a certain highly evolved capacity for devotion. These then attained to where they could receive the Christ-impulse in an advanced degree precisely in this occult school. They could also become clairvoyant in such a way that they became the specially chosen followers of Saint Paul and received the Christ-impulse directly in life.

"Thus, from this school proceeded two groups, as it were, one group which possessed the impulse to carry the teaching of Buddha everywhere, although his name was not mentioned in connection with it, and a second group which, in addition, received the Christ-impulse. Now the difference between these two kinds did not appear very strongly in that particular incarnation, it only appeared in the next. The pupils who had not received the Christ-impulse but who had only gained the Buddha-impulse, became the teachers of the equality and brotherhood of man; on the other hand the pupils who had also received the Christ-impulse, in the next incarnation were such that this Christ-impulse worked up further so that not only could they teach (and they did not consider this their chief task)—but they worked more especially through their moral power.

"One such pupil of the occult school on the Black Sea, was born in his next incarnation as Francis of Assisi (c. 1181–Oct. 3, 1226). No wonder, then, that in him there was the wisdom which he had received, the knowledge of the brotherhood of mankind, of the equality of all men, of the necessity to love all men equally, no wonder that this teaching pulsated through his soul and also that his soul was permeated and strengthened by the Christ-impulse."

Buddha as Wotan

Egyptian Myths and Mysteries, **Rudolf Steiner, Lecture X,** *Old Myths as Pictures of Cosmic Facts,* **Leipzig, September 12, 1908, GA 106**

"Already in Atlantis we meet beings who were among men as our fellows are today; but whom man saw and learned to know when he was in the spiritual world, severed from the body. We have already pointed out how man learned to know Thor, Zeus, Wotan, Baldur as actual companions. By day he lived in the physical world; but in the other condition of consciousness he learned to know spiritual beings who were going through a stage of evolution different from his. In this primeval period of the Earth man did not yet have so solid a body as today; there was as yet nothing like a bony skeleton. The Atlantean body could be seen with physical eyes only to a certain extent. But there were beings who descended only so far as to incarnate in an etheric body. Then there were beings who still embodied themselves at that time, when the air was permeated by water-vapors. When man still lived in the water-fog atmosphere, these incarnations were possible for them. Such a figure was the later Wotan, for example. He said to himself, 'If man incarnates in this fluid matter, then I can also.' Such a being assumed a human form and moved about in the physical world. But as the Earth condensed and man took on ever denser forms, Wotan said, 'No, I shall not go into this dense matter.' Then he remained in invisible worlds, in worlds removed from the Earth.

"This was the general case with the divine spiritual beings. But from then on, they could do something else. They could enter into a sort of connection with men who approached them, who evolved upward from below. We may imagine it thus. Man's evolutionary course was such that he was approaching his lowest point of development. Up to this point the gods had proceeded in company with men. Now they took another path, which was invisible for men on the physical plane. But men who lived according to the directions of the initiates, thereby purifying their finer bodies, approached them in a certain way. A man who was incarnated in the flesh, if he purified himself, could do this in such a way that he could be overshadowed by such a being, who could not descend as far as the physical body. The physical body would have been too coarse for such a being. The result for such a man was that the astral and etheric bodies were permeated by a higher being, which had no other human form for itself; but could enter into another being and proclaim itself through this other being.

"When we are familiar with this phenomenon, we shall not regard incarnation as such a simple matter. There can perfectly well be a person who is the reincarnation of an earlier man, who has developed himself so far and purified his three bodies to such an extent that he is now a vessel for a higher being. Buddha became such a vessel for Wotan. The same being who was called Wotan in the Germanic myths, 1. appeared again as Buddha. Buddha and Wotan are even related linguistically.

"So, we can say that much of what was in the mysteries of the Atlantean time continued in what the Buddha was able to announce. This is in harmony with the fact that what the Buddha experienced is something that the gods had experienced in those spiritual spheres, and that men also had experienced when they were still in those spheres. As the teaching of Wotan thus appeared again, it was a doctrine that paid little attention to the physical plane, emphasizing that the physical plane is a place of woe, and that redemption from it is important. Much of the Wotan-being spoke in the Buddha. Hence it is that stragglers from Atlantis have shown the deepest understanding for the Buddha-teaching. Among the Asiatic population there are races that have remained at the Atlantean level, although externally they must, of course, move ahead with the Earth evolution. Among the Mongolian peoples, much of Atlantis has remained. They are stragglers from the old population of Atlantis. The stationary character in the Mongolian population is a heritage from Atlantis. Therefore, the teachings of the Buddha are especially serviceable to such peoples, and Buddhism has made great strides among them.

"The world moves onward, following its course. One who can look deeply into the evolution of the world does not make choices, does not say that he has more inclination for this or that. He says that what religion a people has is a spiritual necessity. The European population, because it has ensnared itself in the physical world, finds it impossible to feel its way into Buddhism, to identify itself with the innermost teachings of the Buddha. Buddhism could never become a religion for all of humanity. For him who can see, there is no sympathy or antipathy here—*but only a judgment in accordance with the facts*. It would be an error to wish to spread Christianity from a center in Asia, where other peoples are still settled, and Buddhism would be equally false for the European population. No religious view is right if it is not suited to the innermost needs of the time, and such a view will never be able to give a cultural impulse. These are things that we must grasp if we want to understand all the real connections.

"But one should not believe that the historical appearance of the Buddha immediately reveals all that lies within it. If I were to expound all this, I would need several hours. As yet we are far from having unraveled the complications of the historical Buddha. Something still lived in the Buddha. This is not only a being who came over out of the Atlantean time and incarnated in him who incidentally was also a human Buddha. In addition to this something else was contained in him, something of which he could say, 'I cannot yet comprehend this. It is something that ensouls me; but I only participate in it.' This is the Christ-being. This had already ensouled the great prophets. It was a well-known being in the more ancient mysteries, and everywhere and always men had pointed to him who was to come."

Note:

1. Wotan/Odin = Old Norse: Óðinn; the god was also known in Old English as Wōden, in Old Saxon as Uuôden, in Old Dutch as Wuodan, in Old Frisian as Wêda, and in Old High German as Wuotan, all ultimately stemming from the Proto-Germanic theonym Wōðanaz, meaning 'lord of frenzy,' or 'leader of the possessed.'

Christian Rosenkreutz Sends Buddha to Mars

Esoteric Christianity and the Mission of Christian Rosenkreutz, **Rudolf Steiner, Lecture VII,** *The Mission of Gautama Buddha on Mars,* **Neuchatel, December 18, 1912, GA 130**

"…Christian Rosenkreutz [St. John the Divine] was associated with certain other great Individualities concerned with the leadership of humanity. There were present not only personalities in incarnation on the physical plane but entelechies operating in the spiritual worlds; and the Individuality who in the sixth century before Christ had been incarnated as Gautama Buddha also participated.

"The occultists of the East rightly believe—*for they know it to be the truth*—that the Buddha who in his twenty-ninth year rose from the rank of Bodhisattva to that of Buddha, had incarnated then for the last time in a physical body. It is absolutely true that when the individuality of a Bodhisattva becomes a Buddha, he no longer appears on the Earth in physical incarnation. But this does not mean that he ceases to be active in the affairs of the Earth. The Buddha continues to work for the Earth, although he is never again present in a physical body; but sends down his influence from the spiritual world. The 'Gloria' heard by the Shepherds in the fields proclaimed from the spiritual world that the forces of

Buddha were streaming into the astral body of the Child Jesus described in St. Luke's *Gospel*. The words of the Gloria came from Buddha who was working in the astral body of the Child Jesus. This wonderful message of Peace and Love is an integral part of Buddha's contribution to Christianity. But later, too, the Buddha works into the deeds of men—*not physically but from the spiritual world*—and he has co-operated in measures that have been necessary for the sake of progress in the evolution of humanity.

"In the seventh and eighth centuries, for example, there was a very important center of Initiation in the neighborhood of the Black Sea, in which the Buddha taught, in his spirit-body. In such Schools there are teachers who live in the physical body; but it is also possible for the more advanced pupils to receive instruction from one who teaches in an ether-body only. Among the pupils of the Buddha at that time was one who incarnated again a few centuries later. We are speaking, therefore, of a physical personality who centuries later lived again in a physical body and is known to us as St. Francis of Assisi. The quality characteristic of Francis of Assisi and of the life of his monks—which has so much similarity with that of the disciples of Buddha—*is due to the fact that Francis of Assisi himself was a pupil of Buddha.*

"It is easy to perceive the contrast between the qualities characteristic of men who like Francis of Assisi were striving fervently for the Spirit and those engrossed in the world of industry, technical life and discoveries of modern civilization. Many there were, including occultists, who suffered deeply at the thought that in the future two separate classes of human beings would inevitably arise. They foresaw the one class wholly given up to the affairs of practical life, convinced that security depends entirely upon the production of means of nourishment, the construction of machines, and so forth; whereas the other class would be composed of men who, like Francis of Assisi, withdraw altogether from the practical affairs of the world for the sake of the spiritual life. Left to itself, without intervention, history would inevitably have taken this course. But in the wise counsels of the spiritual worlds, steps were taken to avert the worst form of this evil on the Earth.

"A Conference of the greatest and most advanced Individualities was called together by Christian Rosenkreutz. His most intimate pupil and friend, the great teacher Buddha, participated in these counsels and in the decisions reached. At that spiritual Conference it was resolved that henceforward Buddha would dwell on Mars and there unfold his influence and activity. Buddha transferred his work to Mars in the year 1604. And on Mars he performed a deed similar to that performed by Christ on the Earth in the Mystery of Golgotha. Christian Rosenkreutz had known what the work of Buddha on Mars would signify for the whole Cosmos, what his teachings of Nirvāṇa, of liberation from the Earth would signify on Mars. The teaching of Nirvāṇa was unsuited to a form of culture directed primarily to practical life. Buddha's pupil, Francis of Assisi, was an example of the fact that this teaching produces in its adepts complete remoteness from the world and its affairs. But the content of Buddhism which was not adapted to the practical life of man between birth and death was of high importance for the soul between death and a new birth. Christian Rosenkreutz realized that for a certain purification needed on Mars, the teachings of Buddha were pre-eminently suitable. The Christ Being, the Essence of Divine Love, had once come down to the Earth to a people in many respects alien, and in the seventeenth century, Buddha, the Prince of Peace, went to Mars—the planet of war and conflict—to execute his mission there. The souls on Mars

were warlike, torn with strife. Thus, Buddha performed a deed
of sacrifice similar to the deed performed in the Mystery of
Golgotha by the Bearer of the Essence of Divine Love. To dwell
on Mars as Buddha was a deed of sacrifice offered to the Cosmos.
He was, as it were, the lamb offered up in sacrifice on Mars
and to accept this environment of strife was for him a kind of
crucifixion. Buddha performed this deed on Mars in the service
of Christian Rosenkreutz. Thus do the great Beings who guide the
world work together, not only on the Earth; but from one planet
to another.

"Since the Mystery of Mars was consummated by Gautama
Buddha, human beings have been able to receive different forces
from Mars during the corresponding period between death
and a new birth. Not only does a man bring with him into a
new birth quite different forces from Mars; but because of the
influence exercised by the spiritual deed of Buddha, forces
also stream from Mars into men who practice meditation as
a means for reaching the spiritual world. When the modern
pupil of Spiritual Science meditates in the sense indicated by
Christian Rosenkreutz, forces sent to the Earth by Buddha as the
Redeemer of Mars, stream to him.

"Christian Rosenkreutz is thus revealed to us as the great
Servant of Christ Jesus; but what Buddha, as the emissary of
Christian Rosenkreutz, was destined to contribute to the work
of Christ Jesus—this had also to come to the help of the work
performed by Christian Rosenkreutz in the service of Christ
Jesus. The soul of Gautama Buddha has not again been in physical
incarnation on the Earth; but is utterly dedicated to the work of
the Christ Impulse. What was the word of Peace sent forth from
the Buddha to the Child Jesus described in the *Gospel of St. Luke*?
'Glory in the Heights and on the Earth—Peace!' And this word

of Peace, issuing mysteriously from Buddha, resounds from the planet of war and conflict to the soul of men on the Earth.

"Because all these things had transpired, it was possible to avert the division of human beings into the two distinct classes— consisting on the one hand of men of the type of Francis of Assisi and on the other, men who live wholly in materialism."

Earthly and Cosmic Man, Rudolf Steiner, Lecture IX, *Form-Creating Forces—The Principle of Progress in Evolution— Seriousness of the Hour,* Berlin, June 20, 1912, GA 133

"My book *An Outline of Occult Science* describes how, at one time, Sun, Moon and Earth were united in a single planetary existence; the Sun then separated off and, at a later stage, Mercury and Venus; still later, Mars separated off from the Sun. The further we go back in time, the more does such a process become a spiritual process and the question it is essential to understand is really this:— *Who were the Beings who thus separated?* Of primary importance as regards the Earth, was the Christ Being, the great Sun Being Who through the Mystery of Golgotha subsequently united again with the Earth. Thereby all the antecedents of Christianity were brought to a kind of climax and culmination in Christianity itself. With the Mystery of Golgotha, a mighty Cosmic Power streamed into Earth-evolution. It might conceivably be argued that if the Christ came once and once only, this would imply injustice to the souls who lived before His coming. If a materialist were to bring forward such an argument, it might be understandable, but it would certainly not be understandable if it came from a Theosophist. For he knows that the souls living today also lived in earlier times, before the Mystery of Golgotha; the coming of Christ, therefore, is of equal significance for the souls of the pre-Christian ages, because

they all incarnate again in the times following the Mystery of
Golgotha. There is, however, this point to be made and it must be
understood by Theosophists, namely, that in a certain sense the
Buddha forms an exception. We must reach the vantage-point of
the true Buddhist who says that the Individuality in the Buddha
was that of a 'Bodhisattva' who was born as the son of King
Suddhodana, rose in his twenty-ninth year to the rank of Buddha,
thereby attaining a height whence he need no longer return to
a body of flesh. Therefore, that was the final incarnation of the
Bodhisattva Individuality who does not reincarnate in the era
following the founding of Christianity. The lectures in Christiania
1. drew attention to the fact that a very special mission in the
Universe devolves upon an individuality as sublime as the
Buddha. The individuality who became the Buddha had been
sent from the hosts of Christ on the Sun to the 'Venus-men'
before they came to the Earth; the individuality of the Buddha,
therefore, had been sent forth by Christ from the Sun to Venus,
as His emissary. This Individuality came to the Earth with the
'Venus-men' and had thus reached such an advanced stage of
development that through the Atlantean Epoch, on into the Post-
Atlantean Epoch, he was able to attain to the rank of Buddhahood
before the coming of Christ. He was in very truth a 'Christian'
before the time of Christ. We know, too, that later on he revealed
himself in the astral body of the Jesus-Child of St. Luke's *Gospel—
since he no longer needed to return in a body of flesh.* United as
he is with the Christ Stream, a different task devolves upon him
for the times to come. The Buddha need not incarnate again in
a body of flesh. It fell to him to fulfill a certain Deed on Mars—a
Deed not identical with the Mystery of Golgotha; but to be
thought of as a parallel namely—*the Redemption of the people of
Mars.* There is, of course, no question here of a Crucifixion as in

the Mystery of Golgotha; for as may be read in *Occult Science*, the people of Mars are quite differently constituted from human beings on Earth. These things, of course, are the results of occult observation and can only be discovered through clairvoyant investigation.

"Now let us think of this fact—that the Buddha was an emissary of the Christ and had lived on Venus. Then think of the uniqueness of the Buddha-life, of its fundamental character, and proceed as I did myself. First, there came to me the occult knowledge: Buddha goes from Venus to Mars *in order there to accomplish a Deed of Redemption for the beings of Mars.* And now take the life of Buddha and observe how strikingly it differs from the lives of all the other founders of religion in that period. The teachings of all the others tend in the direction of concealing the doctrine of reincarnation; Buddha teaches reincarnation and founds a community based essentially upon piety, upon a kind of remoteness from the world. Ask yourselves whether there are beings for whom this quality would be of fundamental significance—beings whose redemption could be wrought by all that the Buddha had lived through and made his own? If it were possible, now, to say more about the constitution of the Mars beings, you would see that the Buddha-life was a kind of preparation for a higher mission; that it occurred in Earth-existence as a kind of culmination and can have no direct continuation. You may compare much in the Buddha-life with the indications given by occultism and then you will be able to form some real judgment of matters with such far-reaching cosmic connections. To discover them—that will still be beyond you; but you will be able to examine and study them with the help of all the material at your disposal, and you will find agreement and conformity among the indications given. That Buddha is connected with Venus was known, also, to H. P. Blavatsky. In her *Secret Doctrine*, she writes: 'Buddha = Mercury'—'Mercury', because in earlier times the names for Venus and Mercury were confused and reversed. 'Buddha = Venus' would be the proper form. A knowledge possessed by occultists today is already hinted at in H. P. Blavatsky's *Secret Doctrine* 2.—but it must be understood correctly.

"These things are connected with the whole process of advancing evolution. The evolution of man must be studied in connection with the whole universe; man must be thought of as a microcosm within the macrocosm. The fact that Beings do actually mediate between the several planets is entirely in line with these concatenations of cosmic existence, so that a being like the Buddha can actually be regarded as a mediator between planets."

Notes:

1. *Man in the Light of Occultism, Theosophy and Philosophy, Ten lectures given in Christiania (Oslo) June 2-12, 1912 (GA 137)*

2. *The Secret Doctrine, the Synthesis of Science, Religion and Philosophy,* II Vols. by H. P. Blavatsky, Theosophical Publishing Co., Ltd.: London, 1888 (I. Cosmogenesis; II. Anthropogenesis)

The East in the Light of the West, Rudolf Steiner, Lecture IX, The Bodhisattvas and the Christ, Munich, August 31, 1909, GA 113

"We know that in old Indian times men possessed a high degree of clairvoyance in consequence of the relation of the etheric body to the other members; but the time had not then come for this vision to perceive the Christ as anything other than

Vishvakarman [Sanskrit: lit. 'all maker'; the divine architect]—a Spirit in distant regions beyond the sense-world. In the time of the Old Persian civilization, it was first possible dimly to sense the Christ behind the physical Sun. And so it went on. It was possible for Moses to perceive the Christ, as Jehovah, in thunder and lightning that is quite near the Earth. And in the person of Jesus of Nazareth the Christ was seen incarnated as a man. This is the manner of human progress; in the Old Indian Period [7,227 B.C.-5,067 B.C.] wisdom was absorbed through the etheric body, in the Old Persian Period [5,067 B.C.-2,907 B.C.] through the astral body, in the Egypto-Chaldean Period [2,907 B.C.-747 B.C.] period through the Sentient Soul, in the Graeco-Latin Period [747 B.C.-1,414 B.C.] through that which we call the Intellectual Soul. The Intellectual Soul is bound to the world-of-sense. Therefore, it lost the vision of that which extends far, far beyond the sense-world. Accordingly, in the first post-Christian centuries little more of existence was seen than that which lies between birth and death, and that which directly follows as the nearest spiritual region. Nothing was known of that which passes through many incarnations. This was due to the condition of human understanding. Only one part of the life cycle could be made intelligible, man's life on Earth, and the fragment of spiritual life which follows it. That, therefore, is what we find described for the mass of the people. *But that was not to continue.* The outlook of man had to be prepared for an excursion beyond this part of his understanding. Preparation had to be made for a gradual revival of the all-embracing wisdom which man was able to enjoy in the time of Hermes, of Moses, of Zarathustra and of the old Rishis, as well as for offering us the possibility of an ever-increasing understanding of Christ. Christ had to come into the world just at a time when the means of understanding

were most contracted. The way had to be opened for the revival
of the ancient wisdom during the ages to come, and for placing it
gradually in the service of the understanding of Christ. This could
only be accomplished by the creation of Mystery Wisdom. Those
men who came over into and beyond Europe from old Atlantis
brought with them great wisdom. In old Atlantis the majority
of the people were instinctively clairvoyant; they could see into
spiritual realms. This clairvoyance could not develop further; and
withdrew perforce into separate personalities in the West. It was
guided there by a Being who once upon a time lived in deepest
concealment, withdrawn behind those who had already forsaken
the world and who were pupils of the great initiates. This Being
had remained behind in order to preserve for later ages what was
brought over from old Atlantis. Among the great initiates who
had founded mystery places in the West for the preservation of
the old Atlantean wisdom, a wisdom that entered deeply into all
the secrets of the physical body was the great Skythianos, as he
was called in the Middle Ages. And anyone who knows the nature
of the European mysteries knows that Skythianos is the name
given to one of the greatest initiates of the Earth.

"But there also lived in the world for a long, long time,
the Being which in a spiritual sense we may describe as the
Bodhisattva. This Bodhisattva was the same Being who after
completing its task in the West, was incarnated in Gautama
Buddha about six hundred years before our era. This exalted
Being whom, as a Teacher, had by that time withdrawn more
towards the East as a second great Teacher, a second great Keeper
of the Seal of the wisdom of mankind. There was also a third
individuality destined to greatness of whom we have spoken
in various lectures. 1. It is he who was the teacher of the Old
Persians, the great Zarathustra. The three great spiritual Beings

and individualities known to us under the names of Zarathustra, Gautama Buddha and Skythianos are, as it were, incarnations of Bodhisattvas. *For that which lived in them was not the Christ.*

"Mankind had now to be given time to experience in itself the advent of Christ Who had formerly made Himself manifest to Moses upon Mount Sinai; Jehovah was the same Being as Christ, though wearing another form. Time had to be allowed to mankind in which to prepare to receive the Christ. That occurred in the epoch in which the comprehension for such things reached the nadir. But preparation had to be made, in order that understanding and wisdom should again grow greater and greater; and this was part of Christ's mission on Earth.

"There is a fourth individuality named in history behind whom *for those who have the proper comprehension, much lies hidden*—an individuality still higher and more powerful than Skythianos, than Buddha or than Zarathustra. This individuality is Mani [Parthian prophet Mani c. 216-274 A.D.], and those who see more in Manichaeism than is usually the case know him to be a very high messenger of Christ. It is said that a few centuries after Christ had lived on the Earth, there was held one of the greatest assemblies of the spiritual world connected with the Earth that ever took place, and that there, Mani gathered round him three mighty personalities of the fourth century after Christ. In this figurative description a most significant fact in connection with spiritual development is expressed. Mani called these people together to consult with them as to the means of reintroducing the wisdom that had lived throughout the changing times of the Post-Atlantean Epoch and of causing it to unfold more and more gloriously in the future. Who were the personalities brought together by Mani in that memorable assembly? (It should be remembered that such an event can only

be witnessed by spiritual sight.) He called together the personality
in whom Skythianos lived at that time, and also the physical
reflection of the Buddha who had then appeared again, and the
erstwhile Zarathustra who was wearing a physical body at that
time. Around Mani was this council, himself in the center and
around him Skythianos, Buddha and Zarathustra. And in that
council a plan was agreed upon for causing all the wisdom of the
Bodhisattvas of the Post-Atlantean time to flow more and more
strongly into the future of mankind; and the plan of the future
evolution of the civilizations of the Earth was then decided upon,
was adhered to and carried over into the European mysteries
of the Rosy Cross. These particular mysteries have always been
connected with the individualities of Skythianos, of Buddha and
of Zarathustra. They were the teachers in the schools of the Rosy
Cross; teachers who gave their wisdom to the Earth as a gift, *in
order that through it the Christ Being might be understood.* Hence
in all spiritual Rosicrucian schools the deepest reverence is paid
to these old initiates who preserved the primeval wisdom of
Atlantis; to the re-incarnated Skythianos, in whom was seen the
great and honored Bodhisattva of the West; to the temporarily
incarnated reflection of the Buddha; who also was honored as one
of the Bodhisattvas—and finally to Zarathustra, the reincarnated
Zarathustra. They were looked up to as the great Teachers of the
European Initiates. Such presentations must not be taken in the
sense of external history, although they elucidate the historical
course of events better than any external description could do.

"Let me illustrate this statement by saying that there is hardly
to be found a single country in the Middle Ages in which a
certain legend was not everywhere current, though at that time
no one in Europe knew anything of Gautama Buddha, and the
tradition of Gautama Buddha had been completely lost. Yet the

following story was related (it is to be found in many books of the Middle Ages and is one of the widely disseminated stories of that period): Once upon a time there was a King in India to whom a son was born called Josaphat. Extraordinary things were prophesied about this child when he was born. His father therefore especially guarded him; he was only to know what was most precious, he was to dwell in perfect happiness, he was not to become acquainted with pain and sorrow or with the misfortunes of life. He was protected from everything of that sort. It happened, however, that Josaphat one day went out of the palace and passed in succession a sick man, a leper, an aged man, and a corpse—so runs the tale. He returned deeply moved into the king's palace and chanced upon a man whose soul was filled with the secrets of Christianity and whose name was Balaam; Balaam converted Josaphat, and this Josaphat who had experienced all this, became a Christian.

"It is not necessary to bring the Akashic Records to our aid in order to interpret this legend, since ordinary philology suffices to reveal the origin of the name Josaphat. Josaphat is derived from an old word Josaphat; Josaphat again from Joadosaph; Joadosaph from Juadosaph which is identical with Budhasaph—both these last forms are Arabic—and Budhasaph is the same name as Bodhisattva. So, the European occult teaching not only knows the Bodhisattva, it also knows, if it can decipher the name of Josaphat, the meaning of that word. This cultivation of occult knowledge in the West by means of legends contained the fact that there was a time when the being who lived in Gautama Buddha became a Christian. Whether this be a matter of knowledge or not, *it is none the less true.* Just as belated traditions may exist, as men may believe today that which was believed thousands of years ago, and which has been propagated by means of tradition—so they may also believe that it accords with the laws of the higher worlds for Gautama Buddha to have remained the same as he was six hundred years before our era. *But it is not so.* He has ascended, he has evolved and in the true Rosicrucian teachings the knowledge of this fact has been preserved in the form of the above legend.

"Within the spiritual life of Europe, we find him who was the bearer of the Christ, Zarathas or Nazarathos 2.—the original Zarathustra—appearing again from time-to-time; in the same way we meet with Skythianos again and the third great pupil of Mani, Buddha, as he was after he had taken part in the experiences of later ages.

"Thus, the European who had some knowledge of initiation looked into the changing ages and kept his gaze fixed on the true figures of the Great Teachers. He knew of Zarathas, of Buddha, of Skythianos—he knew that through them wisdom was pouring into the civilization of the future-wisdom which had always proceeded from the Bodhisattvas and which must be used in order to promote understanding of the greatest treasure of all comprehension, *the Christ,* Who is fundamentally a completely different Being from the Bodhisattvas and Whom we can understand only by gathering together all the wisdom of the Bodhisattvas. Therefore, in the spiritual wisdom of Europe there is a synthesis of all the teachings that have been given to the world through the three great pupils of Mani and by Mani himself. Even though men may not have understood Mani, a time will come when European civilization will take such form that there will be a feeling for what is connected with the names of Skythianos, Buddha, and Zarathustra. They give to mankind the material whose study will teach us to understand Christ, and through them our understanding of Him will grow more and more complete. The Middle Ages certainly showed a strange form of reverence and worship to Skythianos, to Buddha and to Zarathustra when their names began to percolate through; in certain communities of the Christian religion anyone who wished to be taken for a true Christian had to utter the formula: 'I curse Skythianos, I curse Buddha, I curse Zarathas!' But what it was then thought necessary to curse will become the center for those who will best make Christ comprehensible to man, a central point to which mankind will look up as it did to the great Bodhisattvas through whom the Christ will be understood. Today mankind can at the most bring two things to these teachings of the Rosy Cross—two things which may indicate a beginning of the power and greatness that will appear in the future in the form of the understanding of Christianity, Spiritual Science of today will be the means of making one such beginning, by bringing the teachings of Skythianos, of Zarathustra, of Gautama Buddha to the world again—*not in their old form*—but in an absolutely new form, accessible to investigation from out of its very nature. The elements of what we learn from these three great Teachers must be embodied into civilization. From Buddha, Christianity had to learn the teachings of reincarnation and of Karma; but in the older religion they are to be found in an ancient guise, unsuited to modern times. Why are the teachings of reincarnation and of Karma flowing into Christianity today? Because the initiates have learned to understand them in a modern sense, just as Buddha himself after his fashion understood them —and Buddha was the great Teacher of reincarnation. In the same way we shall attain to an understanding of Skythianos, whose teaching deals not only with the reincarnation of men but with the powers which rule from eternity-to-eternity. So shall the central Being of the world, the Christ, be ever more and more understood. In this way, the teachings of the initiates will gradually flow into humanity.

The spiritual scientist of today can only bring two things in as elementary beginnings compared to what must come about in the future spiritual evolution of mankind. The first element will be that which sinks into our innermost being in the form of the Christ-life; and the second will be an increasingly comprehensive understanding of the Christ by the aid of Spiritual Cosmology. The Christ-life in the inmost heart and an understanding of the world which leads to an understanding of Christ—these are the two elements. We may begin today—for we are only on the threshold of these things, *through having the right feelings.* We meet together for the purpose of cultivating right feelings about the spiritual world and all that is born out of it, as well as right feelings towards mankind. And as we cultivate this right feeling we gradually make our spiritual forces capable of receiving the Christ into our innermost being; for the higher and nobler our feelings become, the more nobly can Christ live within us. We make a beginning by teaching the elementary truths of our Earth evolution, by seeking that which we owe originally to Skythianos, Zarathustra and Buddha and by accepting it as they teach it in our age, in the form they themselves know it, their evolution having progressed to our present age. We have reached a point in civilization now where the elementary teachings of initiation are beginning to be disclosed."

Notes:

1. We are here speaking of these Beings in the spirit in which they were understood by older conceptions of the world, justified today from the standpoint of spiritual science.

2. The 6th c. B.C. incarnation Zarathustra, known as Zaratas or Nazaratos, was a teacher of Cyrus 'the Great,' (Cyrus II of Persia;

c. 600–530 BC; Old Persian: Kūruš), Pythagoras and the Prophet Daniel amongst others.

"The Edict of Restoration, a proclamation attested by a cylinder seal in which Cyrus authorized and encouraged the return of the Israelites to the Land of Israel following his conquest of the Neo-Babylonian Empire, is described in the *Bible* and likewise left a lasting legacy on the Jewish religion due to his role in ending the Babylonian captivity and facilitating the Jewish return to Zion. According to *Isaiah* (45:1) of the Hebrew *Bible*, God anointed Cyrus for this task, even referring to him as a messiah (lit. 'anointed one'); Cyrus is the only non-Jewish figure in the *Bible* to be revered in this capacity." (Wikipedia)

The Vow of the Bodhicitta

It takes great effort and awareness to develop wisdom that can shed light on enlightenment, and personal development, as it relates to the contemporary affairs of the outer world. Spiritual development is about integrating the inner with the outer and finding wisdom in both. To find wisdom, we seek all the places where life springs forth anew. Living-thinking springs from a heart that has 'warmed up' thinking. This higher thinking, referred to by Rudolf Steiner as Moral Imagination, has the power and brilliance to see 'into' things, both within the self and in the outer world around us. Burying our head in the sand or withdrawing into our shell doesn't advance spiritual development; for it is the interaction between the inner (personal) and the outer (other) that quickly develops the soul and spirit.

In Buddhism they call the inner path the 'small boat' and the integration of the inner and outer path the 'big boat.' The small boat (Hinayana) helps the person who cannot control his lower appetites and desires, and it usually requires retreat from the outside world and living in a community of like-minded people who restrict exposure to the temptations of the outer world—where the Seven Deadly Sins run rampant.

This 'hiding' from temptation will not get the practitioner nearly as far as what is called the path of the householder. Householders integrate love, sex, fear, and the many exposures to temptations that could ruin a beginner on the spiritual path of self-development who is seeking enlightenment. Householders work for everyone's enlightenment in the 'big boat' (Mahayana) until all people are helped to ascend to the divine. This dedication to helping others is called the 'Vow of Bodhicitta'—to attain enlightenment for the benefit of all sentient beings.

We have taken the Vow of Bodhicitta and thus must integrate the inner spiritual effort to find Mother Wisdom with the effort to find Her in the living spirit of nature outside of themselves.

Each human being is like a 3D hologram of the universe—a microcosm of the macrocosm. Therefore, the initiate knows that she must find the parts of the Divine outside of her and link them to the parts inside, completing a puzzle that is a copy of the Cosmos itself. Every part of nature that lives and grows has a part of the human soul and spirit inside of it. The wakeful observer watches as the Spirit-Human (Ātman) manifests through life on Earth and follows the cycle of birth, death, and rebirth. This cycle of seeming eternal life is the link to human birth, death, and reincarnation. Nature perfects Herself through evolving each creation into a better and more adaptive living form.

So also, it is with the human being who continues to perfect individualized soul and spiritual virtues into a continuum of incarnations that evolve human qualities into divine qualities that are essentially immortal. This path of enlightenment gives wings to the soul so that it might mount the skies to the spirit.

The awakened soul striving towards the spirit must find the Eternal in all things; and thereby build new worlds through this struggle. Looking out upon the chaos of the geo-political scene in the world and the stress and suffering that can ensue from attempting to integrate it meaningfully into your personal life can leave one empty and looking for answers.

Where do we find solid spiritual ground to stand on in this apocalyptic world that seems to attack us from all directions whether through toxic food, water, air, environment or emotionally through the stress of war, world conflicts, poverty, slavery to debt, painful relationships and failing systems of support from churches, the government, family, and friends?

It seems too bleak to look out of our shells or pull our heads up from a hole in the ground. Trying to figure out the machinations of evil in the hyper-materialistic world gives little time for creating solutions; and, as a result, fatalism can begin to creep in until cynicism forms ever deeper roots within the soul. Subsequently, lethargy sets in and the development of both the inner world and the outer world become something we put on hold because we have problems understanding their meaning and relationship to our own evolution.

The duality of our world is a necessity to develop free and independent consciousness. *It is painful.* When the soul swings between idealism and materialism, it often settles into a lethargic, nihilistic fatalism in the end. In response to this challenging dilemma, it is spiritual development and awakening to our higher consciousness that can serve as a bridge over the chasm of depressing fatalism. Merging the inner world and the outer world is possible once a worldview or cosmology is developed that gives purpose and meaning to human existence by explaining where we came from and where we are going in the future.

We need to begin with the end in mind; for the central task of spiritual development is to merge the spiritual 'within' with the spiritual 'without.' Perhaps the bridge is simply not to fall into fatalism—that nihilistic, agnostic, atheistic, pessimistic attitude of soul that is so prevalent in Western society. Changing fatalism into optimism is accomplished by unfolding an ever-widening view of what it means to be human, and developing a cosmology of who you are and what you plan to become. A cosmology can be seen as a map to guide one on the path back to our home of origin in the Divine. The map is followed by climbing to the highest ground you can find to get a clear perspective of where you are and where you wish to go, then a direct path to the goal can be established for ultimately attaining Spiritual Enlightenment at the summit.

When a spiritual initiate hears of problems in the world, he sees it as an opportunity for growth and advancement. Every horrible situation is an opportunity for the spirit to enter as an antidote. Necessity is the mother of invention and problems are an opportunity for solutions that advance human development.

Evil is here to create an opportunity for good to become stronger. Suffering is here to create the chance to become free of attachment to the outside world. *Every challenge is another opportunity for unfoldment.* When spiritual scientists look upon the outside world and see the many terrible things going on, they see an opportunity to work on their own point-of-view concerning these challenges. When a sacred place is found within, that has been tamed and transformed into an organ of supersensible perception, then a bridge to the outside problem is created and new insight and a new perspective is achieved that may be able to solve the problem, or at least find meaning in it.

It is a passion for integration of the inner with the outer that draws wisdom forth both from within and from without. We eventually find out that the inner is the outer and the outer is the inner. We find our ego in the whole of the Cosmos—as above, so below. If you have created a heaven within your soul and spirit, then it will be possible to create a heaven outside of yourself through direct integration of the spirit in matter, which will then light-up and speak the wisdom that is inherent within its own nature.

We tend to see ourselves everywhere we look, or in other words, project our inner condition upon the outside world. We create the heaven or hell we live in and then ultimately find it in the outer world. The gods and goddesses, as well as heaven and hell can be found within each awakened human spirit. This is the hope of transforming and redeeming our world of matter—through the transformation of our spiritual self. It is this unending interest in the 'other' person and the outside world that is the common characteristic of spiritually advanced beings. True human interest in all things and patience with their development demonstrates the wisdom that has been gleaned from within the human soul and spirit and applied to the outer world.

By using your 'higher self' to understand the confusion of our time brings order and higher meaning to contemporary affairs. The light of spirit, that which is not temporary and temporal, drives the enthusiasm that it takes to find and construct a worldview that illumines the spiritual in both the human domain and the outer world of matter.

For matter is frozen spirit that is re-ignited through consciousness, freedom, and love. When matter is seen for its true nature, it becomes able to return to the spiritual world from whence it came. Humans use matter as a temporary shell within a world of physical substances that fool the human being into believing that matter is the only reality.

When the seeker on the path realizes his/her own immortality through reincarnation, the natural process of birth, death, and rebirth no longer are seen as suffering without meaning in a world of dying matter. When the natural flow of the spirit into and out of matter is understood, wisdom is developed. This wisdom is the antidote for the fatalistic nihilism of materialism. Wisdom can become the foundation to develop faith in the Divine which then makes love, mercy, and grace available to any person who is deeply grateful to the spirit. When this integration of inner and outer is refined into wisdom, heaven can blossom in the soul and in the world.

Wisdom brings with Her the blessings of the Seven Heavenly Virtues that can conquer the Seven Deadly Sins. This process can become a bridge that spans the chasm between idealism and materialism that is found in the duality of modern times played out on the stage of the world as battles between dark brotherhoods with evil agendas and the followers of the Divine – black magicians against white magicians.

Light dispels darkness by its very nature. The brotherhoods of light, the followers of Wisdom have always worked behind the scenes to dispel the darkness of these evil brotherhoods. The battle is both within and without. No one is exempt, and therefore integration with contemporary life is incumbent upon the seeker on the path of spiritual development.

We need to focus on the 'big boat' if we are to create a 'new ark' that can weather the waves of demonic evil and greed that drive the global geo-political scene. We are one globe and one humanity, and it is the job of initiates to engage in the battle and bring illumination to the dark paths of those who wish to fool humans into thinking that it is only 'matter' that exists without any spirit.

Spirit is ready to inspire courage into the willpower of all aspirants who wish to take up the banner of truth, beauty, and goodness and bring Wisdom and Love into the world through freedom. This is a clarion-call to rise-up and face the world with all the strength you can muster to dispel ignorance and create a home for Wisdom in your heart and in the world.

Avatars and Bodhisattvas Guide Us

The word Avatar denotes a 'descent' of a deity into the realm of the human. Hindu deities like Vishnu, Indra, Devi, Shiva, and others were known to 'alight' and make an appearance either through a human being or through a divine vehicle, or Avatar manifested in order to communicate with humankind. Vishnu was known to have incarnated ten different times throughout human history. Buddhism, Jainism and even Christianity have doctrines that are like the Hindu Avatar concept. Christianity embraces the doctrine of a 'savior' who is similar, if not identical, to the doctrine of Avatars.

Avatars descend from a Divine Spiritual World that is eternal into a world that is bound by time. They often mitigate the suffering of humanity and help remove the burden of evil. They also create sacred holy places of refuge against the evils of the world. These highly refined pilgrimage spots represent the preparation of the aspirant to meet the holy teacher or master who lives in the spiritually refined pilgrimage location, sometimes referred to as 'Shambhala.' This is the basis for the tradition that Avatars and spiritual masters live in Shambhala. But whether the Avatars and masters create Shambhala to house their temporal bodies that descend from the higher hierarchies, or they create this rarified etheric realm for aspirants to rise-up to, is determined by the perspective of the aspirant. Shambhala is an etheric realm where even the highest Avatar of all times, Christ, can continuously manifest and provide etheric nourishment for aspirants who can attain that realm.

Avatars are perfected spiritual beings from the higher hierarchy that descend into the earthly realm to assist humanity with its spiritual evolution through attaining virtuous goals that inculcate into human spiritual development the tools that are needed for advancement. Avatars descend from higher realms, whereas masters, bodhisattvas, and Buddhas ascend from the human realm. The highest Avatars are Christ and Sophia. Christ descended from the Holy Trinity and Sophia descend from the realm of the Kyriotetes, the Spirits of Wisdom. It is rare that an Avatar comes down from the pure realms and incarnates in the physical plane. That is why Christ, as an Avatar, will only incarnate in this world once for all times. It is a great suffering for beings of such high vibrations to be limited by a physical body. Sophia, for example, did not incarnate into Mary's physical body; instead, she over-lighted Mary. Sophia descended all the way down to the realm of the Angels from the hierarchical rank of the Kyriotetes, the Spirits of Wisdom.

The greatest Avatar is Christ, according to Rudolf Steiner, since Christ descended from the Holy Trinity, the highest rank of the Divine. Rudolf Steiner tells us in, *The Principle of Spiritual Economy,* Lecture II, *Christianity in Human Evolution: Leading Individualities and Avatar Beings,* Berlin, February 15, 1909 (GA 109):—

"In addition to these leading individualities, who in this sense are like other human beings but stand on a higher plane, there are also other individualities—other beings—who have not gone through various incarnations in the course of human evolution. We can visualize what lies at the bottom of this when we tell ourselves the following: There have been beings in the time of the Lemurian evolution under consideration—beings who no longer needed to descend into physical embodiment as the other human beings just described. They were beings capable of accomplishing their development in higher, more spiritual realms who did not need to descend into corporeal bodies for their further progress. However, in order to intervene in the course of human evolution, such beings can nevertheless descend vicariously into corporeal bodies such as our own. Thus, it can happen that such a being appears; if we test it clairvoyantly in regard to the soul, we cannot say, as we can of other human beings, that we trace it back in time and discover it in a previously fleshly incarnation, then trace it farther back and find it again in another incarnation, and so on. Instead, we will have to admit that in tracing the soul of such a being back through the course of time, we may not arrive at an earlier fleshly incarnation of such a being at all. However, if we do, it is only because the being is able to descend repeatedly in certain intervals in order to incarnate vicariously in a human body.

"Such a spiritual being who descends in this way into a human body in order to intervene in evolution as a human being is called an 'Avatar' in the East; such a being gains nothing from this embodiment for himself and experiences nothing that is of significance for the world. This, then, is the distinction between a leading being that has emanated from human evolution and beings whom we call Avatars. The latter reap no benefit for themselves from their physical embodiments, or even from one embodiment to which they subject themselves; they enter a physical body for the blessing and progress of all human beings. To repeat—an Avatar being can enter a human body just once or several times in succession; but when it does, it is then something different from any other human individuality.

"The greatest Avatar being who has lived on Earth, as you can gather from the spirit of our lectures here, is the Christ—the Being whom we designated as the Christ, and who took possession of the body of Jesus of Nazareth when he was thirty years of age."

There is another type of Avatar incarnation that does not require the Avatar to descend all the way into the physical body. In fact, an

Avatar can 'over-light' a person and influence his etheric body, or other bodies in the nine-fold constitution of the human being. The Being Sophia, Rudolf Steiner tells us, is an Avatar that descended from the realm of the Kyriotetes, the Spirits of Wisdom. Sophia over-lighted Mary, the Mother of Jesus. Sophia only descended into the realm of the etheric body and there Sophia renewed the physical body of Mary with the heavenly Wisdom she brought.

This type of Avatar 'over-lighting' can take place in many different ways. Rudolf Steiner tells us about Shem and the way an Avatar worked through his etheric body and was able to make many copies of it that could be used by others. Rudolf Steiner refers to this type of Avatar over-lighting in the following words:—

The Principle of Spiritual Economy, Rudolf Steiner, Lecture III, *More Intimate Aspects of Reincarnation*, Munich, March 7, 1909, GA 109

"You will remember a personality mentioned in the *Bible*: Shem, a son of Noah and progenitor of the Semitic people. Occult research confirms that there is an individual behind Shem that must be regarded as the tribal individuality of all Semitic peoples. When a number of human beings are to descend from a particular progenitor, a special provision must be made for this in the spiritual world. In the case of Shem, the provision was that an etheric body was specially woven for him from the spiritual world, which he was to carry. This enabled him to bear in his own etheric body an especially exalted being from the spiritual world, a being who could not otherwise have incarnated on Earth because it was incapable of descending into a compact physical body. This being was capable of incarnating only by virtue of the fact that it could now enter the etheric body of Shem. Since Shem had his own physical, etheric, and astral body, as well as his ego, he was first an individual in his own right. Beyond that, however, he was an individual whose etheric body was interwoven with the etheric body of another high being of the spiritual world, specially prepared for the purpose of founding a nation, as characterized above. If clairvoyant perception had confronted Shem, it would have seen Shem himself; but with a second entity extending out of him like a second being, yet still united with Shem's etheric body. This higher being was not Shem; but it incarnated in Shem—the human being—for a special mission. Unlike ordinary human beings, this higher being did not undergo various incarnations; but descended only once into a human body. Such a being is called an Avatar. An Avatar does not feel at home in the world as a human being would; he descends but once into this world for the sole purpose of carrying out a certain mission.

"The part of a human being that is indwelled by such an Avatar being acquires a special character in that it is able to multiply. When a grain of seed is sown into the ground, the stalk grows from it, and the grain is multiplied into the ears of grain. In the same way, the etheric body of Shem multiplied into many copies, and these were woven into all his descendants. That's what happened, and thus the copies of the etheric body that had been specially prepared in Shem as the prototype were woven into the etheric bodies of his direct descendants.

"But this etheric body of Shem was later used in yet another way … Now in the later phase of the evolution of the Semitic people, it became necessary that a very exalted being descend to Earth in order to communicate with them and provide an impetus to their culture. Such a being was the Melchizedek of Biblical history who, as it were, had to 'put on' the preserved etheric body of Shem—the very etheric body that was still inhabited by an Avatar being. Once it was woven into him, Melchizedek was able to transmit to Abraham the impulse necessary for the continued progress of Semitic culture. Here, then, we have become acquainted with another unique way in which an etheric body develops in a particular human being and is subsequently allotted to a specially selected individuality for the fulfillment of a mission."

Rudolf Steiner points out the greatest Avatar of all times, Christ, is able to multiply not only the etheric body, as in the case of Shem— *but also the astral body and the ego or "I Am."* and the transformed astral, etheric, and "I" are all available to be multiplied or serve as imprints from within the realm of spiritual economy as he calls it. In fact, beyond this, Rudolf Steiner points out that by the 7th or Vulcan Planetary Condition Christ will have perfected all nine vehicles, as Macrocosmic Principles.

Many great saints have utilized these perfected bodies of Christ that have been multiplied whenever necessary. For there is no limit to the number of replicas that the perfected bodies of Christ can make. This is described in the following lecture:—

Christianity in Human Evolution, Rudolf Steiner, Berlin, February 15 (GA 109)

"The greatest Avatar being who has lived on Earth is that Being Whom we designate as the Christ, who took possession of the bodies of Jesus of Nazareth in the thirtieth year of his life. This Being, who first came in contact with our Earth at the beginning of our era, Who was incarnated for three years in a body of flesh, and Who since that time has been connected with the astral sphere, the spiritual sphere of our supersensible world—this Being is of unique significance as an Avatar being. We should seek the Christ Being quite in vain in an earlier human embodiment, whereas other, lower Avatar beings can be found to be embodied more than once. They incarnate repeatedly—*but obtain no benefit from their earthly embodiments for themselves.* They only give; they take nothing from the Earth. If you want to understand these things perfectly, you must distinguish between such a lofty Avatar being as the Christ and lower Avatar beings who can have the most varied missions…

"Thus, delicately interwoven are the facts existing behind the physical world that alone make explicable to us what occurs in it. We come to understand history only when we are able to point to such facts of a spiritual nature lying behind the physical ones. History can never be explained by considering physical facts alone.

"What we have been discussing becomes especially significant. Through the descent of an Avatar being the essential soul-spiritual members of the individual who is the bearer of this Avatar being are multiplied and transmitted as copies to other human beings. This fact assumes special significance through the appearance of Christ on Earth. Because the Avatar Being of Christ lived in the body of Jesus of Nazareth, it became possible for his etheric body to be multiplied innumerable times. This was true as well of the astral body and even the ego ["I"]; that is, the ego as an impulse, as it was kindled in the astral body of Jesus of Nazareth when Christ entered his threefold sheath. First, however, we will take into account the fact that through the Avatar Being the etheric and astral bodies of Jesus could be multiplied."

Each Avatar brings the forces from the ranks of the hierarchy where they are usually active, whether angelic, archangelic or the like. Cosmic forces come to Earth along with the Avatar; they descend together to bring help and new life to ailing humanity. These 'visits of the gods' are found in mythology, legends, and religious beliefs worldwide. It is the effort to prepare for the visitation of the gods that the aspirant uses during renunciation and purification that develop moral qualities needed to attract these divine visitations. Zeus came to Earth frequently to interact with humans. Odin traveled about disguised as the 'Grey Wanderer' who might show up at anyone's front door without a moment's notice. Angels came to the house of Lot to save him and his family. But it is usually those who have developed morality and virtue that have a home worthy of a visit from the gods. Avatars come as gods both announced and disguised; it is up to us to recognize their spiritual qualities and open our hearts and homes with unconditional hospitality. Rudolf Steiner explains this in a lecture given in Cologne in 1909:—

The Festivals and Their Meaning II: *Easter*—Lecture VII, *Spiritual Bells of Easter*, pt. I. Cologne, April 10, 1909, GA 109

"As long as the 'I' of man, with its physical expression in the blood, was not seized by an impulse to be found on the Earth, the religions could not teach of the force of self-redemption in the human 'I.' So, they describe how the great spiritual Beings, the Avatars, descend and incarnate in human bodies from time to time when men are in need of help. They are Beings who for the purpose of their own development need not come down into a human body, for their own human stage of evolution had been completed in an earlier world-cycle. They descend in order to help mankind. Thus, when help was needed, the great God Vishnu descended into earthly existence...

"The all-powerful Divinity can be proclaimed in no more beautiful or more sublime words than these. The Godhead seen by Moses in the element of fire, Who not only weaves and surges through the world as a macrocosmic Divinity, is to be found, too, *within* man. Therefore, in all beings who bear the human countenance, Krishna lives as the great Ideal to which the innermost essence of man develops from within. And when, as was the goal of ancient wisdom, man's breath can be spiritualized through the impulse given by the Mystery of Golgotha—*this is the redemption that is achieved by what now lives within ourselves.* All the Avatars have brought redemption to mankind through power from above, through what has streamed down through them from spiritual heights to the Earth. But the Avatar Christ has redeemed mankind through what He gathered out of the forces of mankind itself, and He has shown us how the forces of redemption, the forces whereby the Spirit becomes victor over matter can be found *in ourselves.*

"Thus, although through the spiritualization of his breath he had made his body incorruptible, even Kashiapa with his supreme enlightenment could not yet find complete redemption. The incorruptible body must wait in the secret cave until it is drawn forth by the Maitreya Buddha (successor to Buddha). Only when the 'I' has spiritualized the physical body to such a degree that the Christ Impulse streams into the physical body, is the miraculous cosmic fire no longer needed for redemption; for redemption is now brought about by the fire quickened in man's own inner being, in the blood."

The Principle of Spiritual Economy, Lecture VIII, The Event of Golgotha—The Brotherhood of the Holy Grail—The Spiritualized Fire, Cologne, April 11, 1909, GA 109

"The external expression for the ego 1. is the blood. That is a great secret, but there have always been human beings who were acquainted with it and who were aware of the fact that copies of the ego of Jesus of Nazareth are present in the spiritual world. And since the Event of Golgotha, there have always been human beings through the centuries who had to see to it that humanity matured slowly to the point where some individuals could accept copies of the ego of Jesus Christ, just as some human beings received copies of His etheric or astral body. A secret way had to be found to preserve this ego in a silent, deep Mystery until the time when a suitable moment for its use would be at hand. To preserve this secret, a brotherhood of initiates was formed: The Brotherhood of the Holy Grail. This brotherhood goes back to the time when, as is reported, its founder took the chalice that Christ Jesus had used at the Last Supper and collected in it the blood that dripped from the wounds of the Savior when He was hanging on the cross. This founder of the brotherhood collected the blood of Christ Jesus, the expression and copy of His ego, in the chalice that is called the Holy Grail. It was kept in a holy place—in the brotherhood—that through its institution and initiation rites comprised the Brothers of the Holy Grail.

"Today the time has come when these secrets can be revealed because the hearts of human beings can become ripened through spiritual life to an extent where they elevate themselves to an understanding of this great mystery. If Spiritual Science can kindle souls so that they warm up to an engaged and lively understanding of such mysteries, these very souls will become mature enough, through casting a glance at that Holy Grail, to get to know the mystery of the Christ-Ego—the eternal ego into which any human ego can be transformed. This mystery is a reality. All that people have to do is to follow the call by Spiritual Science to understand this mystery as a given fact so that they can receive the Christ-Ego at the mere sight of the Holy Grail. To accomplish this, it is necessary only that one understand and accept these happenings as fact.

"At a future time when people will be increasingly well-prepared to receive the Christ-Ego, it will imbue the souls of human beings to an ever-increasing degree so that they can strive upward to approach the position where their great model Christ Jesus used to be. Only through this process will human beings learn to understand in what respect Christ Jesus is the great model of humanity, and only then will they begin to understand that the certainty and the truth of the life everlasting emanates from the corpse on the wooden cross at Golgotha. Those Christians of the future who are inspired and imbued by the Christ-Ego will also understand something that was formerly known to no one but the illuminates. Not only will they understand the Christ who has gone through death, but they will also understand the triumphant Christ of the *Apocalypse*, who's coming was previously prophesied and who arose from the dead into the spiritual fire. And Easter can always be to us a symbol of the risen Christ, a connecting link from the Christ on the cross to the triumphant, risen, elevated Christ who draws all human beings upward as He sits at the right side of the Father.

"The Easter symbol opens a perspective not only on the future of the entire Earth but also on that of human evolution. Easter is our assurance that someday the human beings inspired by Christ will increasingly change from Saul to Paul individuals and become more and more capable of seeing a spiritual fire. To be sure, just as Christ appeared to Moses and to those who had declared their faith in Him in the physical fire of the bramble-bush and in the lightning on Sinai as a prophecy of His own coming, so will He appear to us in the spiritualized fire of the future. 'He is with us every day to the end of the world,' and to those who allowed their perception to be illuminated by the Event of Golgotha, to those He will appear in the spiritual fire even if at first, they had seen Him in a different form.

"Since Christ exerted such a profound influence on all aspects of earthly life, as far down as the human skeleton, that which formed His mortal body out of the elements of the Earth also cleansed and sanctified all substances on the Earth to such an extent that the world can never again become what the Wise Men of the East sadly feared it would forever be. They believed that the illuminate of the future, the Maitreya-Buddha, would be unable to find people on Earth who could rise to an understanding of him because they would have sunk too deeply into the material world.

"Christ was led to Golgotha to sublimate matter and redirect it to spiritual heights and to prevent fire on Earth from becoming slag instead of spiritualized essence. When human beings themselves are spiritualized, they will again understand the primeval wisdom of the spiritual world from which they have formerly come. And thus, after human beings have gone through an even deeper understanding, the Maitreya-Buddha will find on Earth an appreciation that otherwise he would have been unable to encounter. We understand everything that we learned in our youth better after we have become more mature through our trials and after we can look back upon the experiences of our youth. Similarly, mankind will understand the primeval wisdom of the world by looking back at it in the light of Christ and through the Event of Golgotha.

"And now, how can the imperishable remains of Kashyapa be saved, and for what destination are they being saved? It is written that the Maitreya-Buddha will appear and touch him with the right hand, and then the corpse will be removed in a fire. The fire that Paul saw on the way to Damascus was the same wonderful, spiritualized fire within which the body of Kashyapa will be safely transported upward; and in this fire everything great and noble of ancient times will be saved. We will see the forces of the past that were sublime, magnificent, and full of wisdom stream and flow into what humanity has gained as a result of the Mystery of Golgotha."

Note:

'I' is often translated into English as 'Ego' from the original German: 'Ich'. This German word 'Ich' we know from Rudolf Steiner was first coined by the initiate Ulfilas;† when he first began Gothic as a written language; which subsequently became the German language.

> "Through Christianity much that is of a communal nature has been brought about, which previously was not communal. The active power of this substitution is expressed in the fact that through inner vision, through true mysticism, community with Christ is possible. This has also been embodied in language. The first Christian initiate in Europe, Ulfilas, himself embodied it in the German language, in that man found the 'Ich' within it. Other languages expressed this relationship through a special form of the verb, in Latin for instance the word 'amo,' but the German language adds to it the Ich. 'Ich' is J. Ch. = Jesus Christ. It was with intention that this was introduced into the German language. It is the initiates who have created language. Just as in Sanskrit the AUM expresses the Trinity, so we have the sign ICH to express the inmost being of man. By this means a central point was created whereby the tumultuous emotions of the world can be transformed into rhythm. Rhythm must be instilled into them through the Ich. This center point is literally the Christ."

> **Rudolf Steiner, *Foundations of Esotericism*, Lecture II,**
> **September 27, 1905, GA 93a**

† Ulfilas (c. 311-383) was a 4th century preacher of
Cappadocian Greek descent. He was the apostle to the Gothic
people; who oversaw the translation of the *Bible* into Gothic.
Known as the *Gothic Bible* or *Wulfila Bible* is the Christian
Bible in the Gothic language spoken by the Eastern Germanic
(Gothic) tribes in the Early Middle Ages. During the third
century, the Goths lived on the northeast border of the Roman
Empire, in what is now Ukraine, Bulgaria and Romania. During
the fourth century, the Goths were converted to Christianity,
largely through the efforts of Bishop Wulfila, who is believed to
have invented the Gothic alphabet. The translation of the *Bible*
into the Gothic language is thought to have been performed in
Nicopolis ad Istrum in today's northern Bulgaria. Traditionally
ascribed to Wulfila.

An Avatar may have a special connection to an evolving Bodhisattva, who will one day become a Buddha. The Maitreya Bodhisattva,
who is evolving into the Maitreya Buddha, has a special connection
with the greatest Avatar Christ. Maitreya is mirroring or copying the
bodies of Christ that are available to multiply for great initiates in the
etheric realm, or realm of spiritual economy. The Maitreya is so filled
with the aspects of the Christ Avatar that he resembles him in all ways.
Rudolf Steiner speaks of this in Milan in 1911:—

Buddha and Christ: The Sphere of the Bodhisattvas, **Rudolf Steiner, Milan, September 21, 1911, GA 130**

"The utterances of the Maitreya Buddha will be permeated in a
miraculous way with the power of Christ. Occult investigations
show us today that in a certain respect even the external life
of the Maitreya Buddha will be patterned on the life of Christ.
In ancient times, when a great Individuality appeared and was
to become a teacher of humanity, signs indicating this showed

themselves in the early youth of the child in question, in special talents and qualities of soul. There is however, a different kind of development in the course of which a complete change in the personality becomes apparent at a certain point in his life. What happens is that when this human being has reached a certain age, his ego is taken out of his bodily sheaths and a different ego passes into his body. The greatest example of this is Christ Jesus Himself, of whom in his thirtieth year the Christ-individuality had taken possession. All the incarnations of the Bodhisattva who will become the Maitreya Buddha have shown that in this sense his life will resemble that of Christ."

There are many ranks of beings above the human being. The teachings from the Esoteric Christian school of Bishop Dionysius the Areopagite (*Acts* 17:34), that was established by St. Paul in Athens, count them as nine ranks; but other older religions have untold ranks of beings from the Creator to the elementals below our feet. There are many ways that other beings can work in our physical realm and not be 'human,' even though they use human intelligence to do their work. Through the teachings of Rudolf Steiner we hear about these beings and when they evolved, or didn't, in cosmic history. In *The Spiritual Guidance of Mankind* we read about a few of these ranks of hierarchical beings and their relationship to humanity.

The Spiritual Guidance of Mankind, Rudolf Steiner, Lecture II, Copenhagen, June 7, 1911, GA 15

"The ancient Egyptians still remembered a time when the leading personalities of the nation were clearly conscious of their connection with what are called gods, angels, or dhyanic beings. Now what sort of beings were these, who were not incarnated in a human form of flesh and blood, but who influenced mankind. They were man's predecessors, advanced beyond the human stage.

"There is in these days much misuse of a word which may in this connection be applied in its true meaning, the word 'Superman.' If we really wish to speak of 'Supermen,' it is these beings who may rightly be so called. Humans during the Old Moon evolution, the planetary stage preceding our Earth, had now outgrown humanity. They were only able to appear in an etheric body to clairvoyants. It was thus that they came down to Earth from spiritual worlds and ruled here even as late as Post-Atlantean times…

"The dhyanic or angelic beings proper, who are the great inspirers of humanity, and to whom the Egyptian referred as being still their teachers, did not appear in human bodies. They could only manifest themselves *through* human beings. On the other hand, the beings in a mid-position between men and angels were still able, in very early times to incarnate in human bodies. Hence amongst the human race inhabiting the Earth in the Lemurian and Atlantean Epochs, we find people whose innermost soul-nature was that of an angel in a backward state. Not only ordinary people were going about the Earth, who through their successive incarnations were to arrive at the ideal of humanity; but beings who only outwardly appeared like them. These had to bear a human body; for the outward form of a human being in the flesh is dependent on earthly conditions. Especially in more ancient times did it happen that beings belonging to the lowest category of Luciferic individualities were present amongst men. And so, at the same time that the angel-beings were working on human civilization through man, Lucifer-beings were also incarnated and founding human civilizations in various places. And when in the old folk legends, it is related that in some place there lived a great man who was the founder of a civilization we are not to understand that such a Lucifer-being was necessarily the vehicle of evil; but rather that human civilization was to receive countless blessings from him."

Not only are there beings from the past that have relationships with humanity, but there are also the beings of the future that are now coming into our realm to teach and guide us directly as Avatars have in the past. These beings are also 'descending' to the Earth to help humanity spiritually evolve. These "future supermen and superwomen" descend as we ascend to meet them in the middle. It is out of the future that these beings come, bearing the gifts of humanity's future spiritual development. These beings tell us who we will become as we climb the ranks of the spiritual hierarchies ascending to become angels and beyond.

Rudolf Steiner refers to these beings with the names of the future states of the incarnations of the Earth—Mercury (second half of the Earth incarnation), Venus, and Vulcan. He later refers to these beings as 'our older brothers and sisters.' These beings can be seen as various manifestations of "futuristic" Avatars.

Materialism and the Task of Anthroposophy, Rudolf Steiner, Lecture XIV, Dornach, May 13, 1921, GA 204

"Thus, since the eighties of the nineteenth century, heavenly beings are seeking to enter this Earth existence. Just as the Vulcan men were the last to come down to Earth, [This occurred during the Atlantean Epoch] so Vulcan beings are now actually entering this Earth existence, and it is thanks to the fact that these beings from beyond the Earth are bringing messages down into this earthly existence that it is possible at all to have a comprehensive Spiritual Science today.

"Taken as a whole, however, how does the human race behave? If I may say so, the human race behaves in a cosmically rude way toward the beings who are appearing from the Cosmos on Earth, albeit, to begin with, only slowly. Humanity takes no notice of them, ignores them. It is this that will lead the Earth into increasingly tragic conditions. For in the course of the next few centuries, more and more spirit beings will move among us whose language we ought to understand. We shall understand it only if we seek to comprehend what comes from them, namely, the contents of Spiritual Science. *This is what they wish to bestow on us.* They want us to act according to Spiritual Science; they want this Spiritual Science to be translated into social action and the conduct of earthly life.

"Since the last third of the nineteenth century, we are actually dealing with the influx of spirit beings from the Universe. Initially, these were beings dwelling in the sphere between Moon and Mercury; but they are closing in upon Earth, so to say, seeking to gain a foothold in earthly life through human beings imbuing themselves with thoughts of spiritual beings in the Cosmos. This is another way of describing what I outlined earlier when I said that we must call our shadowy intellect to life with the pictures of Spiritual Science. That is the abstract way of describing it. The description is concrete when we say:—

Spirit beings are seeking to come down into Earth existence and must be received.

Upheaval upon upheaval will ensue, and Earth existence will at length arrive at social chaos if these beings descended and human existence were to consist only of opposition against them. For these beings wish to be nothing less than the advance guard of what will happen to Earth existence when the Moon reunites once again with Earth.

"Nowadays it may appear comparatively harmless to people when they think only those automatic, lifeless thoughts that arise through comprehension of the mineral world itself and the mineral element's effects in plant, animal, and man. Yes, indeed, people revel in these thoughts; as materialists, they feel good about them; for only such thoughts are conceived today. But imagine that people were to continue thinking in this way, unfolding nothing but such thoughts until the eighth millennium when Moon existence will once more unite with the life of the Earth. What would come about then? The beings I have spoken about will descend gradually to the Earth. Vulcan beings, Vulcan supermen, Venus supermen, Mercury supermen, Sun supermen, and so on will unite themselves with Earth existence. Yet, if human beings persist in their opposition to them, this Earth existence will pass over into chaos in the course of the next few thousand years. People will indeed be capable of developing their intellect in an automatic way; it can develop even in the midst of barbaric conditions. The fullness of human potential, however, will not be included in this intellect and people will have no relationship to the beings who wish graciously to come down to them into earthly life."

Now that we have reviewed Rudolf Steiner's indications on Avatars in the selections above, let's look at what he wrote and said about the greatest of all Avatars, Christ. A broader selection follows:—

The Principle of Spiritual Economy, Rudolf Steiner, Lecture II, Christianity in Human Evolution—Leading Individualities and Avatar Beings, Berlin, February 15, 1909, GA 109

"Today we shall proceed a little further and speak again about more complicated questions of reincarnation or re-embodiment.

To that end, we must first realize that differences exist among the beings who occupy leading places in the Earth's human evolution. In the course of earthly evolution, we must distinguish those leading individuals who have developed along with humanity from the beginning, but who have made more rapid progress. Some have made relatively slow progress through their incarnations and still have long distances to travel in the future. But there are also souls who have developed rapidly, who, one might say, have utilized their incarnations to better advantage and are therefore at a stage of soul-spiritual development that will be attained by normal men only in the far distant future. Nevertheless, we may say that however advanced these individual souls may be, however far they may tower above normal men, they have still followed the same path in earthly evolution as the rest of humanity but have merely advanced more rapidly.

"Besides these leading individualities, who in this sense are like the rest of humanity but are at a higher stage, there are also other individualities, other beings, who have by no means gone through various incarnations as other men have in the course of their evolution. We can perhaps illustrate what lies at the bottom of this by saying that there were beings in the time of the Lemurian evolution who no longer needed to descend so deeply into physical embodiment as the other men who have just been described. There were beings who could have accomplished their development in higher, more spiritual regions and who did not need to descend into bodies of flesh for their further progress. In order to intervene in the course of human evolution it is nevertheless possible for these beings to descend vicariously, so to speak, into just such bodies as our own. At any time, therefore, a being may appear of whom, if we make the necessary clairvoyant test, we cannot say, as we can of other human beings, that we trace the soul back in time and find it in a previous fleshly incarnation, trace it farther back and find it again in another incarnation, and so on. Instead, we must say that if we trace the soul of such a being back through the course of time, we may perhaps not find it at all in a former fleshly incarnation. If we do, it is only because the being in question is able to descend repeatedly to incarnate vicariously in a human body."

"A spiritual being who descends thus into a human body in order to intervene in evolution as a human being; but without gaining anything from this embodiment for himself or experiencing anything here in the world of special significance for himself, is called an Avatar. This is the distinction between a leading being who has sprung from human evolution itself and an Avatar. An Avatar being reaps no benefits for himself from his physical embodiments, or from even one embodiment to which he may subject himself; he enters a physical body for the blessing and advancement of mankind. Thus, an Avatar being can either enter a human body just once or several times in succession, and when embodied is entirely different from other human beings…

"…Through the descent of an Avatar being the essential soul-spiritual members of the individual who is the bearer of this Avatar being are multiplied and transmitted as copies to other human beings. This fact assumes special significance through the appearance of Christ on Earth. Because the Avatar Being of Christ lived in the body of Jesus of Nazareth, it became possible for his etheric body to be multiplied innumerable times. This was true as well of the astral body and even the ego; that is, the ego as an impulse, as it was kindled in the astral body of Jesus of Nazareth when Christ entered his threefold sheath. First, however, we will take into account the fact that through the Avatar Being the etheric and astral bodies of Jesus could be multiplied…

"Now, through the appearance of the Christ principle in earthly evolution one of the most significant phenomena in humanity occurred. What I have told you about Shem is fundamentally typical and characteristic of the pre-Christian times. When an etheric or an astral body is multiplied in this way, the copies are transmitted as a rule to those people who are related by blood to the one who had the original. Hence, the copies of Shem's etheric body were transmitted to the members of the Hebrew tribe. This was changed when the Christ Avatar Being appeared. The etheric and astral bodies of Jesus of Nazareth were multiplied, and the copies preserved until they could be used in the course of human development. They were not, however, limited to any one nationality nor to any particular people. But when in the course of time a human being appeared who, irrespective of nationality, was ripe to have interwoven with his etheric or astral body an etheric or astral copy of the etheric or astral body of Jesus of Nazareth, they could be woven into his being. Thus, we see how it became possible in the course of time for all sorts of people to have woven into them copies of the astral or etheric bodies of Jesus of Nazareth…

"What made it possible for a number of people in those centuries to be able to receive revelations, which were in a certain sense clairvoyant, concerning the events in Palestine? It was possible because the multiplied copies of the etheric body of Jesus of Nazareth had been preserved and were woven into a great number of people. They were able to wear them as garments that were woven into their etheric bodies. This was not Jesus' own etheric body, but copies of the original. In these centuries there were those who could possess such an etheric copy and who could thereby have a direct knowledge of Jesus of Nazareth and the Christ…

"Francis of Assisi, for example, was such a personality. This fact becomes explicable when we, as people of the present, study his life and are unable to understand his conscious ego; but are nevertheless compelled to hold the deepest possible reverence for the entire world of his feelings and for all that he did. He was one of those who had a copy of the astral body of Jesus of Nazareth, and it was this that made his accomplishments possible. Many of his followers in the Order of the Franciscans also had such copies interwoven with their astral bodies.

"All the strange and otherwise mysterious phenomena of that time will become luminous and clear to you, if you bring properly before the eyes of your soul this mediation in world evolution between that time and the past. It is also important to know, however, whether what was woven into these people of the Middle Ages from the astral body of Jesus of Nazareth was more from what we call the Sentient Soul, the Intellectual Soul or the Consciousness Soul, since the astral body must, of course, be considered in a certain sense as something containing all of this as well as enclosing the ego. All that was woven into Francis of Assisi was wholly Sentient Soul of Jesus of Nazareth. Wholly Sentient Soul of Jesus of Nazareth was also contained in that remarkable personality, Elizabeth of Thüringen, who was born in 1207. Knowing this secret of her life will enable you to follow her biography with your soul. She, too, was a personality who had a copy of the astral body of Jesus of Nazareth woven into her Sentient Soul. The riddle of the human being is solved for us by means of just such knowledge.

"One phenomenon above all will become understandable when you know that during this time the most diverse personalities had Sentient Soul, Intellectual Soul or Consciousness Soul woven into them as copies of the astral body of Jesus of Nazareth. From this you will be able to comprehend that little understood science, scholasticism. What task did the scholastics set for themselves? They set out to find on the basis of judgment and intellect, verifications and proof of that with which there was no historical connecting link, and which was no longer available with the direct clairvoyant certainty that existed in previous centuries through the interwoven etheric body of Jesus of Nazareth. Then, from the Intellectual Soul, that is, from the intellectual element of the copy of the astral body of Jesus of Nazareth, they set themselves the task of proving with subtle and clearly developed concepts all that existed in their literature as mystery truths. Thus arose the strange science in which an attempt was made to achieve what was perhaps the ultimate in human intellect. One may think of the content of scholasticism as one wishes; but simply by means of this delicate discrimination and exact outlining of concepts, the capacity for human reflection was developed and impressed upon the culture of that period. This capacity to think with acute and searching logic through scholasticism was implanted into humanity between the thirteenth and fifteenth centuries.

"Among those who were more imbued with the copy of what had constituted the Consciousness Soul of Jesus of Nazareth, the special conviction arose, because the ego ["I"] functions in the Consciousness Soul that the Christ can be found in the ego. Because they had within them the element of the Consciousness Soul from the astral body of Jesus of Nazareth, the inner Christ rose resplendent in their souls. These are the individuals whom you know as Meister Eckhart [c. 1260-c. 1328], Johannes Tauler [c. 1300-Jun. 16, 1361] and all the other bearers of medieval mysticism.

"Here you see how the diversified phases of the astral body were multiplied because the exalted Avatar Being of Christ had entered into the body of Jesus of Nazareth, and they worked on in the following age to bring about the real development of Christianity. This was an important transition in other respects also. We have seen how in the course of its development humanity was dependent upon having incorporated within it copies of the other bodies of Jesus of Nazareth. In the early centuries there were people who were entirely dependent upon the physical plane; then in the following centuries came those to whom the etheric body of Jesus of Nazareth was accessible to interweave with their etheric bodies. Later, between the twelfth and fourteenth centuries, people tended more toward the astral body, the bearer of power and judgment, and so the astral body of Jesus of Nazareth came to be incorporated in them...

"What, then, has happened since the sixteenth century? The ego has come gradually into prominence, and with it human egotism, and with egotism, materialism. What the ego had previously acquired was unlearned and forgotten and it became necessary for man to limit himself to what the ego can observe, to what the physical sensory system is able to give to ordinary intelligence. That alone could the ego take into the inner sanctuary. The civilization since the sixteenth century is one of egotism. What must now enter into this ego? Christian evolution has passed through a development in the physical, etheric and astral bodies, and has penetrated as far as the ego. Now it must take into this ego the mysteries and secrets of Christianity. Following a time when the ego learned to think through Christianity and to apply the thoughts to the outer world, it must now be possible for it to be made into a Christ receptive organ. It must rediscover the primordial wisdom of the

Great Avatar, Christ. By what means must this come about? By a more profound understanding of Christianity through Spiritual Science. Having been carefully prepared through the three stages of physical; etheric and astral development, the concern should now be that the organ within man be opened so that he may henceforth see into his spiritual environment with the eye that can be opened for him by the Christ.

"As the greatest Avatar Being, Christ descended to Earth. Let us view this in the right perspective and try to look at the world as we shall be able to see it when we shall have received the Christ into ourselves. We then find the whole process of our world evolution illuminated and pervaded by the Christ being. In other words, the Christ and Christianity must become the perspective center of the cosmic view.

"So, you see how Christianity has gradually prepared itself for what it is to become. In the early centuries the Christian received Christianity with his physical capacity for knowledge, later with his etheric capacity, and throughout the Middle Ages with his astral capacity. Then for a time Christianity in its true form was repressed until the ego had been trained by the three bodies in the course of Christian development. But since this ego has learned to think and to direct its vision to the objective world, it is now capable also of seeing in all phenomena spiritual facts that are intimately connected with the Central Being, *the Christ*. It is capable of beholding the Christ everywhere in the most varied forms as the foundation of the objective world."

"Here we stand at the starting point of spiritual scientific comprehension and knowledge of Christianity. We begin to understand the task and mission that has been assigned to this movement for spiritual knowledge, and we come to realize its reality. The individual human being has physical, etheric and astral bodies, and ego, and continues to rise to ever more lofty heights; it is the same in the historical development of Christianity. We might say that it, too, has physical, etheric and astral bodies, and an ego—*an ego that can even deny its origin*—as in our time, since it can become egotistic. But it is still an ego that can receive the true Christ Being into itself, thereby rising to ever higher stages of existence. What the human being is in particular, the great world is in its totality, and that includes its historical development. When observed in this light, a perspective of the far-distant future opens before us from the spiritual scientific viewpoint, and we realize how it can lay hold upon our hearts and fill them with meaning. We comprehend evermore what we have to do, knowing that we are not groping in the dark. We have not devised ideas that we intend arbitrarily to project into the future; but we intend to harbor and to follow only those ideas that have been slowly prepared through the centuries. It is true that, after the physical, etheric, and astral bodies had come into existence, the ego appeared and is now to be developed little by little up to Spirit-Self, Life-Spirit and Spirit-Human. It is also true that modern man, with his ego form and present thinking could only be developed from the astral, etheric, and physical forms of Christianity. Christianity has now become ego. Just as truly as this was the development of the past, so it is also true that the ego form of humanity can appear only after the astral and etheric forms of Christianity have been developed. Christianity will develop on into the future. It will offer humanity far greater things and the Christian development and standard of life will arise in new form. The transformed astral body will appear as the Christian Spirit-Self; the transformed etheric body will appear as the Christian Life-Spirit. In a radiant perspective of the future of Christianity, Spirit-Human shines forth before our souls like a star toward which we strive, illuminated and glowing through and through with the spirit of Christianity."

As to the deeper significance of the Christ Event that came about through the Mystery of Golgotha, it is best to let Rudolf Steiner explain this in his own words. To do this it was thought judicious to include a complete lecture; therefore, as before, it won't be surrounded by quotation marks, but rather it will be preceded and followed by a triangle.

$$\Delta$$

Cosmic I and Human I, Rudolf Steiner, Lecture XIII, Munich January 9th, 1912 (CW 130)

It is necessary that we speak somewhat further this evening concerning the nature of Christ Jesus. This necessity arises from the fact that at the present time there is much discussion of this subject, especially in Theosophical circles, and on that account the need confronts us in a very real sense to come to complete clarity upon many a point in this domain.

Today we shall have to discuss an aspect of the question which to many may perhaps appear somewhat strange; but it is very important nevertheless. We will start with the evolution of man. We know, of course, that this has progressed in such a way that the whole of humanity within our Earth evolution passes through certain cyclic Periods. And we have often spoken of the fact that we can distinguish Five Cultural Periods, up to and including our time, since that great catastrophe which we call the Atlantean catastrophe [7,227 B.C.], through which life on the old Atlantean continent was transformed into life on the new continents—that is, our life. We speak of the first, the ancient Indian Cultural

Period; of the second, the great ancient Persian Period; of the third, the Egypto-Chaldaic-Babylonian; and of the fourth, the Greco-Latin, which, for a more comprehensive worldview, only receded, let us say, between the eighth and the twelfth Christian century; and then we speak of our own, the present, the fifth post-Atlantean Period, since 1413.

Now, human souls—hence the souls of all of you sitting here—have gone through various incarnations in these successive [2,160 year] Cultural Periods up to the present time, one soul in many embodiments, another in a relatively smaller number. These souls, according to the characteristics of the Periods, appropriated this or that from their experiences, brought it with them from the earlier into the later incarnations, and then appeared as souls at a stage of development dependent upon what they had previously experienced in the different Cultural Periods.

But now we can also speak of the fact that, of the various members of man's nature, generally one or another; but usually a definite member, was formed and developed in each Cultural Period—but note well that this was only generally the case. Thus, we can say that if human beings permit to work upon them all that our Period of civilization can give, they are especially called in our time to develop what in our spiritual scientific movement we call the Consciousness Soul; whereas, during the Greco-Latin Period the Intellectual or Rational Soul was preeminently developed; during the Egypto-Chaldean-Babylonian Period, the Sentient Soul; during the Old Persian Period, the Sentient or Astral Body; and in the Old Indian, what we call the Etheric or Life Body. These various members of man's nature have come to their corresponding development in connection with individual souls passing through these Cultural Periods, in one or, in most cases, in several incarnations. And in that Period which will follow our own as the sixth Post-Atlantean Period, that member will be especially developed which we characterize as Spirit-Self, and which in theosophical literature has been designated Manas; and in the last, the seventh Post-Atlantean Period, that which we characterize as Life-Spirit, and which in Theosophical literature is called Budhi; while Spirit-Man, or Atma, is to be evolved only in a far distant future, after another catastrophe.

And so, in the present and the near future, we are in the midst of the development through our environment, through the normal conditions of our civilization, of what is called the *Consciousness Soul.*

But now we know that this entire development of the human being, this evolution of the individual soul members as we differentiate them, is essentially bound up with something else— is essentially bound up with the gradual incorporation of the human ego. *For this incorporation of the human ego into the nature of man is the whole mission of the Earth evolution.* So we have, as it were, two intermingling evolutionary streams, in that we must go through the Earth evolution, following that of the Old Saturn, Old Sun and Old Moon [Planetary Conditions], and that as Earth humanity we bring to development especially this fourth member, the Ego ["I"], and join this Ego to the other principal members of human nature, upon which preparatory work was done earlier: namely, the physical body, the etheric body, and the astral body. You must now distinguish this great, most important evolutionary stream, which is connected with the great embodiments of our Earth planet itself, from the smaller evolutionary stream, which I have previously characterized as playing its part within so short a time as the Post-Atlantean Epoch [7,227 B.C.-7,894 A.D.].

No one who has understood the matter up to this point should ask the question: Then how does it happen that man had already

developed the etheric or life body, on the Old Sun, and that now
a special development of the same body should take place during
the ancient Indian Period? Anyone who has understood really
should not ask this question; for the facts are these: To be sure,
preliminary work was done upon the etheric or life-body during
the Old Sun; man came upon the Earth already in possession of
an etheric body. But this body can now be more finely formed;
it can be worked upon by the later members which man has
developed. So that naturally man's etheric body is at a relatively
high stage when he is incarnated in an ancient Indian body; but in
this [First] Post-Atlantean Period he works upon his etheric body
with the ego which he has acquired—with all that the human
being has meanwhile gained for himself, he works upon it and
refines it. And it is essentially a refining of the various members of
man's nature which takes place in our Post-Atlantean Epoch.

If you now take the entire evolution and consider what has
just been said, the fourth post-Atlantean Period, the Greco-Latin
[Cultural Period 747 B.C.-1,414 A.D], will appear to you quite
especially important; for what we call the Rational or Intellectual
Soul had then to be worked upon and brought to a more
refined form within the human being. But by that time the Ego,
which belongs to the greater evolutionary stream, had already
undergone a particularly high development. So we can say that
up to the fourth Post-Atlantean Period, the Greco-Latin time, this
ego of man had evolved to a certain stage, and it was incumbent
upon it then to work upon the Rational or Intellectual Soul; and
in our time upon the Consciousness Soul.

You see in a certain sense there now exists an intimate
relationship between the human ego and the three members of
man's soul nature: the Sentient Soul, the Rational or Intellectual
Soul, and the Consciousness Soul. Chiefly within these three

members the human ego lives its inner life; and in our fifth post-Atlantean Period [5th Cultural Period 1,414 A.D.-3,574 A.D.] it lives in the Consciousness Soul, and will live most deeply in it, because in the Consciousness Soul the pure ego can come to expression quite unhindered, so to speak, by the other members. Indeed we live in our time in the Cultural Period in which this ego has the great and special mission of developing itself, of building upon itself.

If we take a sort of prophetic glance into the future, at what is to come, if we say that man will develop the Spirit-Self, or Manas, in the next, the sixth Post-Atlantean Period [6th Cultural Period 3,574 A.D.-5,734 A.D.], then we recognize that Spirit-Self, or Manas, really lies above the sphere of the ego. As matter of fact, man could not in the future develop the Spirit-Self out of his own forces; but if he is to develop his Spirit-Self, he must be helped in a certain way by that which flows to the Earth through the forces of higher Beings. Man has come to that stage in the evolution of his ego where, out of his own forces, he really can develop only up to the Consciousness Soul; but this development would not be complete if he should not anticipate in a certain sense that which will reach its true, complete, self-impelled human evolution only upon Jupiter, the next embodiment of our planet. Up to the end of the Earth evolution man should develop his ego; and he will have had opportunity to accomplish this development within the Sentient, Intellectual, and Consciousness Souls. But the actual Spirit-Self is to become the human possession only upon Jupiter; only there will it become the fitting human endowment. On Jupiter man will have about the same relation to the Spirit-Self that he has to the ego on Earth. If then the human being develops the Spirit-Self during the Earth-period, he cannot relate himself to it as to the ego. Of our ego we say:—

We ourselves are that; it is ourselves in reality.

When in the next stage, the sixth Post-Atlantean [Period], the Spirit-Self shall have come to expression, then we shall not be able to address this Spirit-Self as ourselves; but we shall say:—

Our ego has developed to a certain stage, so that our Spirit-Self can shine into it, as from higher worlds, as a kind of Angel Being, which we ourselves are not; but which shines into us and takes possession of us.

Thus will our Spirit-Self appear to us; and only upon Jupiter [Planetary Condition] will it appear as our own being, as our ego now is. *Human evolution moves forward in this way.*

Hence, in the next, the sixth Post-Atlantean Period, we shall feel as if drawn upward to something which shines into us. We shall not say:— Thou Spirit-Self within me ... but we shall say:— I, partaker in a Being who shines into me from upper worlds, who directs and leads me, who, through the grace of higher beings, has become my guide! ... That which will come to us only upon Jupiter [i.e., Future 5th Planetary Condition] as our very own, we shall feel in the sixth Period as a kind of guide shining upon us from the higher worlds ... And thus it will be later with the Life-Spirit, or Budhi, with the Spirit-Man, and so on ... So a time will come when man will speak of himself otherwise than he does now. How does one speak of himself now when he speaks in the sense of Spiritual Science? He says:— I have three sheaths, my physical body, my etheric body, and my astral body. Within these I have my ego, the essential Earth possession, which is evolving within these three sheaths. These sheaths are, as it were, my lower nature; I have grown beyond it, I look down to this, my lower nature; and I see in what my ego has become a preparatory stage of my own being, which will grow and evolve further and further ... In the future man will have to speak otherwise; then he will say:— I have not only my lower nature and my ego; but I have a higher nature, to which I look up as to something which is a part of me in the same way as my sheaths, which I have from earlier stages ... So in the future the human being will feel that he is placed midway, so to speak, between his lower and his higher nature. The lower nature he already knows now; the higher will in the future appear as if standing above him, just as now the lower is below him. So we may say that man grows from his fourth to his fifth, sixth and seventh principles during the Earth evolution—*but his fifth, sixth and seventh principles will not be his direct possession during the actual Earth evolution*—but something to which he will gradually attain. The matter must actually be conceived in this way.

We shall have to experience a time when we shall say:— *Certainly it was our Earth mission to develop our ego. But with prophetic anticipation we see something which is to come to development in us on Jupiter.*

What we are now experiencing during our Earth evolution: namely, that we permeate ourselves, so to speak, with a human ego nature; and that during the past Earth-time up to the present we have developed a finer fashioning of our lower principles; and that we shall perfect the higher principles in the future—all that we as human beings experience on Earth, more advanced beings whom we designate as Angels, or Angeloi, experienced upon earlier planetary embodiments. But also the higher members of the Hierarchy, the Archangels, or Archangeloi, and the Archai, have had this experience upon the earlier embodiments of our

Earth planet, upon Old Moon, Old Sun and Old Saturn. For them also there was at that time a kind of fourth member which they developed; and then in the second half of the corresponding planetary embodiments, they anticipated that which actually is to come to full development in them upon the Earth, as with us the Spirit-Self will come to development on [Future] Jupiter. They had not at that time fully embodied it within themselves as their possession—*but they looked up to it.*

If in the first place we look back to the Old Moon evolution, we must speak of beings who during that time should have reached their seventh principle, in exactly the same way that we human beings during the Earth evolution come to the seventh principle—that is, not to embody it completely—*but to look up to it.* When we speak of Luciferic beings, we refer to those who during the Old Moon evolution remained in the condition in which a man would be who, during the Earth evolution, had not brought to full development his fifth, sixth and seventh principles—but had turned aside from such development; who perhaps had stopped with the fourth or with the fifth. That is, those beings who were at the very diverse stages of Luciferic beings were not fully evolved. So, we can say that human beings came over from the Old Moon evolution to Earth evolution. They came over in such a way that those who completed the Old Moon evolution brought with them a normal development: their physical body, etheric or life body, and astral body; and on the Earth, quite properly, they should develop the ego, into which they should then take up the other principles. Other beings who stand higher than man should already have developed on the Old Moon what for them corresponds to the human ego. But they could have brought this Old Moon ego to full development only if they had anticipated what for them would be fifth, sixth, and seventh principles, of which they should have fully developed the fifth on Earth. They should have reached their seventh principle; but these Luciferic beings did not do so. They barely evolved the fifth or sixth; and thus, did not stop with the fourth, but they did not bring the fourth to full development, because they did not anticipate the fifth, sixth and seventh principles—*but stopped with the fifth or sixth.*

We distinguish then two classes of these Old Moon beings: First, those who had developed only their fifth principle, so that they were as we human beings would be if we should develop the Spirit-Self in the sixth Post-Atlantean Period, and then stop, and not develop the sixth and seventh principles. Let us keep in mind this one class, who as Luciferic beings had developed their fifth principle; and then note another class of Old Moon beings of the Luciferic sort who had developed their sixth principle but not their seventh. There were such at the beginning of the Earth evolution, when man began the development of his ego. So we can ask:— What was the situation as regards these beings at the beginning of the Earth evolution? There were beings there who eagerly expected to develop their sixth principle during the Earth evolution, beings of a Luciferic kind, who upon the Old Moon had evolved only as far as their fifth principle and wished to develop their sixth upon the Earth. And there were beings of the second class, who had already developed their sixth principle on the Old Moon, and who wished to develop their seventh on the Earth. *They expected that of the Earth evolution.* Then there was man, who came over with three principles, to develop his fourth.

So, we can distinguish human beings waiting for opportunity to develop their ego, Luciferic beings expecting to evolve their sixth principle, and the Luciferic beings who would evolve their seventh. We shall disregard those who were ready to develop their fifth, but there were such.

Now you see we have distinguished three classes, so to speak, of microcosmic Earth beings, three classes of beings who arrived upon the scene of Earth evolution. Of the three classes, however, only one could win a physical body for itself on the Earth; for the conditions which the Earth presents for the development of a physical fleshly body can be furnished only in conformity with its entire earthly relationship to a fourth human principle. Only that being could acquire a physical body for himself who wished to develop his fourth principle as ego. The other beings, who wished to develop a sixth and a seventh principle, could not get physical bodies for themselves. For there is no possibility on the Earth for the direct acquisition of physical human bodies for beings who come into this Earth evolution so unadapted to it. The possibility does not exist for the direct acquisition of such a physical body. What did these beings have to do? They had to say to themselves:—

Of course we cannot have direct access to a human physical body consisting of flesh and bones, for such bodies are for human beings who wish to develop their ego. Hence we must take refuge in a kind of substitute physical body; we must search for human beings who belong to the most highly developed, that is, those who have evolved, let us say, their fourth principle. We must creep into these human beings, and in them our nature must work in such a way that they will be enabled to form their sixth or seventh principle...

The consequence of this was that among the ordinary human beings of ancient times some appeared who could be *possessed* by higher Luciferic beings. These naturally stood higher than man, since they were to form their sixth or seventh principle, and man only his fourth. Such higher beings of a Luciferic kind went about on the Earth in earthly human bodies. They were the leaders of Earth humanity; they knew and understood much more, and could do much more than other men. We are given accounts of these beings in ancient tales and legends, and it is told of them that here and there they were founders of great cities, were great leaders of peoples, and so on. They were not merely normal men upon Earth; but they were men who were possessed by such higher beings of a Luciferic sort—*possessed in the best sense of the word*. We can only understand human Earth evolution when we take account of such things.

But especially the less highly evolved of these beings, because they cannot get human bodies for themselves, are always trying to continue their evolution in the bodies of human beings. And that is just what we have been able to characterize. Luciferic beings always had the longing to continue their evolution in the way described, by *possessing* human beings; and *they are still doing that today*. Lucifer and his hosts work in the human soul; *we are the stage for the Luciferic evolution*. While we human beings simply take the human earthly body in order to develop ourselves, these Luciferic beings take us and develop *themselves in us*. And that is the temptation of human beings that the Luciferic spirits work in them.

But meanwhile these Luciferic spirits have advanced, just as human beings have advanced; so that very many of them who, let us say, when man entered upon the Atlantean time, stood on the threshold ready to evolve their sixth principle, are now already forming their seventh, although of course this evolution on the Earth is abnormal. Such a spirit accomplishes this in the following way: He takes possession of a man, perhaps for only a few years, in order to make use of the experiences of this man, who on his part is thus furthering his own evolution. This is nothing evil in human nature; for since we can bring the Consciousness Soul to expression in our time, we can be possessed by Luciferic spirits who are evolving their seventh principle. What does a person become when he is possessed by such a lofty Luciferic spirit? A genius! But because as man he is possessed, and the real human nature is irradiated by this higher being, he is impractical for ordinary accomplishments—*but works in some one realm as a pioneer and a leader.*

One may not speak of the Luciferic spirit as if he were something altogether hateful; but because he develops himself as a parasite by entering the human being, he causes the man possessed by him and under his influence to work as a man of genius, as if inspired. So the Luciferic spirits are absolutely necessary, and the gifted men of Earth are they in whom the Luciferic spirit is working diligently—generally only for a couple of years. If that were not the case, Eduard Schuré would not have been able to describe Lucifer sympathetically 1.; for Lucifer is actually assigned a share in the great cultural progress of the Earth, and it is narrow-mindedness in traditional Christianity to see in the Luciferic being only the wicked devil—this signifies nothing less than gross Philistinism ... "Nature is sin, Spirit is devil; they cherish between them Doubt, their deformed bastard child," we read in *Faust*. Certainly it is fitting for the narrow, traditionally-formed Christianity to call Lucifer the devil, and to hate him; but he who has an understanding of human evolution knows that the Luciferic principle works in the genius. It is fitting for the spiritual scientist to look these things straight in the face. And we should have no inducement whatever to rise to our fifth and sixth principles, if these spirits did not push us forward. It is the Luciferic spirits to whom we really owe the forward thrust, given because they seek thereby their own evolution, and through which we ourselves are enabled to grow out beyond our ego. It is said trivially that poets and geniuses and artists grow above the narrowly confined human ego.

So, we look up to the Luciferic spirits in a certain way as to leaders of men. We must free ourselves from narrowness, from all orthodox Christianity which calls Lucifer only a devil worthy of hatred. We must recognize the liberating character of the Luciferic principle, which has also been ordained by the good gods; for it drives us out beyond ourselves during the Earth evolution, so that we prophetically anticipate what will come to us as our own possession only during Jupiter, and so on. Thus there actually exists upon Earth a reciprocal influence of microcosmic beings, who were present at the beginning of the Earth evolution—such a reciprocal influence that human beings are led forward, while they are developing their own ego, by beings related to them in such a way that it must be admitted that they are higher than man; for they have evolved their fifth principle and are developing their sixth, or are already evolving their seventh, while man is working only upon his fourth. So in these Luciferic beings we see superhuman beings—microcosmic superhuman beings.

And now we will turn aside from these spiritual beings whom we regard as Luciferic, and consider the *nature of Christ*.

The Christ is quite radically different from other beings who share in the Earth evolution. He is a Being of quite another order; He is a Being who remained behind, not only during the Old Moon evolution, as the Luciferic spirits did; but who, foreseeing the Old Moon evolution, actually remained behind still earlier, namely, during the Old Sun evolution; and it was from a certain assured wisdom far above the human that He remained behind during the Old Sun evolution. We cannot regard this Being as microcosmic in the sense which applies to the other beings we have been considering; for we have to regard as microcosmic beings those who were connected with this Earth evolution from its beginning. The Christ was not directly connected with the Earth evolution—*but with the Sun evolution*. He was a *macrocosmic Being* from the beginning of the Earth evolution on, a Being who was exposed to entirely different conditions of evolution from those of the microcosmic beings. And His evolutionary conditions were of a special sort; they were such that this macrocosmic Christ Being evolved the macrocosmic ego ['I'] outside earthly conditions. For this Christ evolution it was normal to bring to ego-perfection, outside the Earth, an ego of a macrocosmic sort, and then to descend to Earth. And so, for the evolution of the Christ Being it was normal, when He descended from the macrocosm to our Earth, to bring into it the great impulse of the macrocosmic ego, in order that the microcosmic ego, the human ego, might take up this impulse, and be able to go forward in its evolution. It was normal for the Christ to have the macrocosmic ego-impulse—not the microcosmic ego-impulse— just as much evolved as man upon the Earth had developed the microcosmic. Thus, the Christ Being is a Being Who in a certain sense is like the human being, only that man is microcosmic and has brought his four principles to expression microcosmically, and hence has his ego also microcosmically as Earth-ego—but the Christ as Cosmic-Ego. His evolution was such that He was great and significant because of the perfect development of this ego, which He brought down to Earth. And He had not the fifth macrocosmic principle, and not the sixth; for He will evolve these on Jupiter and on Venus [future Planetary Conditions], in order that He may give them to man.

The Christ, then, is a four-membered Being, including His macrocosmic ego, just as man himself is microcosmically a four-membered being. And as man during the Earth time has as his mission the development of his ego, in order to be able to *receive*, so the Christ had to develop His Ego, in order to be able to *give*. When He descended to Earth His whole being was employed in bringing His fourth principle to expression in the most perfect possible form. Now each macrocosmic principle has an inner relationship to the corresponding microcosmic principle; the fourth macrocosmic principle in the Christ corresponds to the fourth microcosmic principle in man, and the fifth in the Christ will correspond to the Spirit-Self in man.

Thus, the Christ entered upon His earthly course in that He brought down to man out of the macrocosm what man was to evolve microcosmically—only the Christ brought it as a macrocosmic principle. He entered the Earth evolution in such a way that during its course He would not have a fifth, sixth and seventh principle as His personal possession, just as man in his way does not possess them.

The Christ is a Being Who had evolved macrocosmically up to the fourth principle, and the evolution of His fourth principle during the Earth course consists in His bestowing upon man everything which will enable him to evolve his ego.

If we take a complete survey, we have at the beginning of Earth evolution three classes of beings: human beings who were to bring their fourth principle to full development on Earth; a class of Luciferic beings who were to evolve their sixth principle; and a class of Luciferic beings who were to develop their seventh principle—beings who, because they were ready to develop their sixth and seventh principles, stood higher than man,—in fact, ranged far above man in this respect. But they also ranged above Christ in this regard; for the Christ was to bring His fourth principle to expression on the Earth, in devotion to humanity. It will not be the Christ, let us say, that will quicken man in the future to bring to expression something other than the True Ego, the innermost human being—to reach ever higher and higher stages. It will be the Luciferic spirits who will lead man out beyond himself in a certain sense.

Anyone who looks at the matter superficially can say: 'Of course then the Christ stands lower than, for example, the Luciferic spirits.' ... because the Christ came to Earth with something which is fully related to man's fourth principle. For that reason, He is not at all fitted to lead man above himself; but only more deeply into his own soul being. He is fitted to lead the individual soul-being of man more and more *to itself.* The Luciferic beings have evolved the fourth, fifth and sixth principles, and hence in a certain way stand higher than the Christ. Practically, that will work out in the future so that through the admission of the Christ principle into human nature, this human nature will become more and more deepened, will take up more and more light and love into its own being; so that the human being will have to feel *Light* and *Love* as belonging to his very self. The immeasurable deepening of the human soul—*that will be the gift of the Christ Impulse, which will work on and on forever.* And when the Christ shall come, as that coming has been represented in many lectures, then He will work only upon the deepening of human souls. The other spirits who have higher principles than the Christ, though only microcosmic principles, will in a certain sense lead man out beyond himself. The Christ will deepen the inner life of man—*but also make him humble.* The Luciferic spirits will lead man out beyond himself, and make him wise, clever, talented—*but also in a certain sense haughty—*

will teach him that he might become something superhuman even during the Earth evolution. Everything, therefore, which in the future shall lead man to rise above himself, as it were, which will make him proud of his own human nature even here upon Earth—*that will be a Luciferic impulse*; but what makes a man more deeply sincere, what brings his inner life to such depths as can come only through the complete development of the fourth principle—*that comes from the Christ.*

People who look at the matter superficially will say that Christ really stands lower than the Luciferic beings; for He has developed only the fourth principle, and the others, higher principles. Only the difference is that these other beings bring the higher principles as something parasitic, grafted upon human nature; but the Christ brings the fourth principle in such a way that it penetrates human nature, takes root within it, and fills it with *power*. As the fleshly body of Jesus of Nazareth was once permeated and empowered by the fourth macrocosmic principle, so will the bodies of those who take the *Christ into themselves* be permeated by the fourth macrocosmic principle. Just as the fourth macrocosmic principle is the gift of Christ, so will the sixth and the seventh principles be the gifts of the Luciferic spirits. So that in the future—and such time is now being prepared for—we may experience that people lacking in understanding will say:— If we examine the *Gospels*, or otherwise allow to work upon us what Christ gave to humanity, we see that in regard to His teaching He does not at all rank as high as perhaps do other spiritual beings who are connected with humanity ... They are higher than man in a certain way. They cannot penetrate the entire man, but they take root in his *intellect*, they make him a *genius*! And one who observes only outwardly says that these beings stand higher than the Christ ... And the time will come when the most powerful, the

most significant of these Luciferic spirits, who will wish to lead
the people out beyond themselves, so to speak, will be extolled,
and looked upon as a great human leader; and it will be said that
what the Christ was able to furnish was really only a bridge. Now
already there are people who say:— What do the teachings of
the *Gospels* amount to! We have outgrown them.—As has been
said, men will point to a lofty, versatile spirit, a spirit of genius,
who will take possession of a human fleshly nature, which he will
permeate with his genius. It will be said that he surpasses even the
Christ! For the Christ was one who gave opportunity to develop
the fourth principle; but this one gives opportunity during the
Earth evolution to attain to the seventh principle.

Thus will the Christ Spirit and the spirit of this being face one
another—the *Christ Spirit*, from whom humanity may hope to
receive the mighty macrocosmic impulse of its fourth principle,
and the *Luciferic Spirit*, who will wish in a certain way to lead
humanity beyond this.

If people would agree that we must acquire from the Luciferic
spirits only that to which we can look up in the same way that we
look down to our lower nature ... then they would be doing right.
But if people should come to say: You see the Christ gives only the
fourth principle, while these spirits give the sixth and seventh ...
people who think thus concerning Christ will worship and extol
... the *Antichrist*.

Thus will the position of the Antichrist towards the Christ
make itself felt in the future. And with the outer intellect, with the
outer wisdom, one will not be able to challenge such things; for it
will be possible to produce much which from the point-of-view
of the intellect and talent will be more clever in the Antichrist
than that which will more and more flow into the soul from the
Christ, as the highest human principle. Because Christ brings to

man the fourth macrocosmic principle—since it is macrocosmic, it is infinitely more important than all microcosmic principles; it is *stronger* than they, even though it is related to the human ego, stronger than all others which can be gained during Earth evolution—still, because it is only the fourth principle, it will be thought of as lower than the fifth, sixth and seventh, which come from the Luciferic spirits; and especially lower than that which comes from the Antichrist.

It is important that, upon the basis of Spiritual Science, it should be perceived that this is so. In regard to the Copernican theory, which has set the Earth in motion, as it were, has snatched it from the repose in which it had earlier been placed, and has led it around the Sun; which has shown how the Earth is a grain of dust in the universe—in regard to this theory it is asked: How can the Christian idea exist alongside this! A contradiction is constructed between the Christian thought and this natural science, because it is said that in olden times men could look up to the cross on Golgotha and to Christ; for the Earth seemed to them as the place chosen out of all the Universe, and the other cosmic bodies seemed small to them, and really existing for the sake of the Earth. The Earth then appeared to man—so it could be said—worthy to bear the cross of Golgotha! But when the Copernican theory laid hold upon the spirits of men, they began to scoff and to say:— The other cosmic bodies must have at least an equal significance with the Earth, so the Christ must have passed from one cosmic body to another; but since the other world bodies are much larger than the Earth, it would really be strange that the God-man should accomplish His work of redemption on the little Earth! A Scandinavian scholar actually said this. He was of the opinion that, with the Christ drama, it was just as if a powerful drama were presented on a little stage in a suburb, or in a village theater, instead of being presented on a great stage in a capital city. He said:— 'It is absurd that the greatest drama in the world should not be performed upon a great cosmic body. It is exactly as if a great production should not be given in a splendid theater, but in a miserable village theater!'

Such a speech is, of course, very peculiar; but we can reply that the Christian legend has taken care that nothing so foolish could be said; for it has not even laid the scene of this drama in a splendid place on Earth—*but only in a poor stable*. That fact already shows that no such objection should be made as that of the Scandinavian scholar. People do not consider how inconsequential they are with their peculiarly wise thoughts. The idea has no effect in the presence of the great simple truth which is given in the Christian legend. And if this Christian legend lays the scene of the birth of Jesus, not in a splendid, important capital city of the Earth—but in a poor stable, then it does not seem absurd that, in contrast to the greatest cosmic bodies, the Earth should have been chosen as the place to bear the cross. In general, the method by which the Christian teaching in its way sets forth what the Christ had to bring to humanity, is an indication of that great teaching which Spiritual Science is to give to us again today. If we allow the *Gospels* to work upon us—we can search there for the deepest truths of Spiritual Science, as we have often seen—but how are these great truths contained in the *Gospels*? Well, I might say that if those people who have not a spark of the Christ Impulse in them are to rise to an understanding of what is in the *Gospels*, they must absolutely rack their brains—there must even be a certain genius developed! From the fact that so few people understand the spiritual scientific interpretation of the *Gospels*, even in the smallest degree, it can be gathered that the normal human consciousness is not capable of it. Through

Luciferic forces, with the development of genius, the *Gospels* can be understood in a purely superficial way; but as they are presented, how do these truths confront us? They come to us as if they gushed forth—the most perfect and highest good—directly from the Being of Christ—without effort or exertion of any kind—and speaking in such a way to hearts which allow themselves to be permeated by the Christ Impulse, that souls are illuminated and warmed through and through. The way in which the greatest truths are there presented to man is the opposite of the clever method. The method in the *Gospels* takes account of the fact that in the direct, original, elemental way in which these truths gush forth, perfect, from the fourth macrocosmic principle in Christ Jesus, they pass over immediately to the people. Indeed, care has even been taken that the cleverness of man, the sagacity of all the Luciferic influence in human evolution, shall give much sophistical explanation of these words of Christ, and that we shall only gradually be able to win through to their simplicity and grandeur, to their fundamental character. And as with the words of Christ, so also with the facts concerning Christ.

If we present such a fact, let us say, as the Resurrection, by means which Spiritual Science provides, what strange fact do we there confront? A very important German Theosophist said, even in the third decade of the 19th century, that it can be seen how the human intellect is being more and more permeated by the Luciferic principle. This was Troxler. He said that the human intellect was utterly Luciferic in all that it comprises. It is generally difficult to make direct reference to the deeper theosophical truths; but those of you who attended my course of lectures in Prague 2. will recall that I referred to Troxler at that time, in order to show how he already knew what can now be taught concerning the human etheric body; he said that the human intellect is permeated by the Luciferic forces. If we today, disregarding the Luciferic forces, wish to comprehend the resurrection with good theosophical forces, then we must point to the fact that at the baptism by John in the Jordan something significant occurred: that then the three bodies of the Luke Jesus boy were permeated by the macrocosmic Christ Being, Who then lived for three years on Earth, and then these bodies passed through the Mystery of Golgotha with this Christ Being. The development of Christ Jesus during the three years was naturally different from that of other men. We must inquire concerning this development, so that, going into fundamental facts, and with the principles of Spiritual Science, we may comprehend what the resurrection actually was.

Jesus of Nazareth stood by the Jordan. His ego ["I"] separated from the physical body, the etheric body and the astral body, and the macrocosmic Christ Being came down, took possession of these three bodies, and then lived until the 3rd of April of the year 33—as we have been able to determine. But it was a different kind of life; for, beginning from the baptism, this life of Christ in the body of Jesus of Nazareth was a slow process of dying. With each advancing period of time during these three years, something of the sheaths of Jesus of Nazareth died away, so to speak. Slowly these sheaths died, so that after three years the entire body of Jesus of Nazareth was already close to the condition of a corpse and was only held together by the power of the macrocosmic Christ Being. You must not suppose that this body in which the Christ dwelt was like any other body—let us say a year and a half after the John baptism in the Jordan 2.; it was in such a state that an ordinary human soul would have felt at once that it was falling away from him—because it could only be held together by the powerful macrocosmic Christ Being. It was a constant, slow dying, which continued for three years.

And this body had reached the verge of dissolution when the Mystery of Golgotha took place. Then it was only necessary that those people mentioned in the narrative should come to the body with their strange preparation of spices and bring about a chemical union between these special substances and the body of Jesus of Nazareth, in which the macrocosmic Christ Being had dwelt for three years, and then that they should place it in the grave. Very little was needed then to cause this body to become dust; and the Christ Spirit clothed Himself with an etheric body condensed, one might say, to physical visibility. So, the risen Christ was enveloped in an etheric body condensed to physical visibility; and thus He went about and appeared to those to whom He could appear. He was not visible to everyone—*because it was actually only a condensed etheric body which the Christ bore after the resurrection*; but that which had been placed in the grave disintegrated and became dust. And according to the latest occult investigations, it is confirmed that there was an earthquake. It was astonishing to me to discover, after I had found from occult investigation that an earthquake had taken place—that this is indicated in the Matthew *Gospel*. The Earth divided and the dust of the corpse fell in and became united with the entire substance of the Earth. In consequence of the violent shaking of the Earth, the clothes were placed as they were said to have been found, according to the description in the John *Gospel*. It is wonderfully described in the *Gospel of St. John*.

In this way we must understand the Resurrection occultly, and we need not at all come into contradiction with the *Gospels*. I have often called attention to the fact that Mary Magdalene did not recognize the Christ when He met her. How could one possibly fail to recognize again someone whom he had seen only a few days before, especially if he were such an important personality as Christ Jesus was? If it is said that Mary Magdalene did not know Him, then He must have appeared to her in another form. She recognized Him only when she heard Him speak. Then she became aware of Him.

For all the details of the Gospels are entirely comprehensible occultly. But someone might say that Thomas was challenged by the risen Christ, when He appeared to the disciples, to feel the scars with his hands ... then it must be supposed that the scars were still there—that Christ had come to the disciples with the same body which had been resolved to dust. No! Imagine that someone has a wound: then the etheric body contracts in a special way and forms a kind of scar. And in the specially contracted etheric body; from which were drawn the constituents of the new etheric body with which the Christ clothed Himself, these wound-marks were made visible—were peculiarly thickened spots ... so that even Thomas could feel that he was dealing with a reality.

This is a remarkable passage in the occult sense. It does not in any way contradict the fact that we have to do with an etheric body, condensed to visibility by the Christ force; and that then also the Emmaus scene could occur. We find it described in the *Gospel*, not as an ordinary receiving of nourishment; but a dissolution of the food directly by the etheric body—*through the Christ forces*—without the cooperation of the physical body.

All these things can be understood today through occult principles, on the basis of Spiritual Science. Apart from the poorly translated passages, the *Gospels* can be understood literally in a certain way. Everything becomes clear in a wonderful way, and anyone who has grasped this will say to himself, when he notices a contradiction: 'I am too stupid for this.' He does not feel that he is so clever as the modern theologians, who say: '*We* are not able to comprehend the Resurrection as it is described in the *Gospels!*' ... But we can comprehend it exactly thus, when we understand the principles.

How does all that has now been said work upon human reason? Well, it affects people in such a way that they say:— 'If I am to believe the Resurrection, then I shall have to set at naught all that I have gained up till now through my reason. That I cannot do. Therefore, the Resurrection must be effaced.'

The reason which speaks thus is so permeated by Lucifer that it cannot comprehend these things. Such a reason will come to reject more and more the great, effective, elementary language and facts of earlier times, and those connected with the Mystery of Golgotha. But Spiritual Science will be called upon to comprehend these things, even to the smallest details. It will not reject that which, as fifth, sixth, and seventh principles, can transcend the fourth macrocosmic principle. Nevertheless, it will see in the fourth macrocosmic principle *the greatest impulse which has been given to the Earth evolution.*

But from this you see that in a certain way it is not exactly easy to understand the Christ evolution within the Earth, because in a sense the objection is justified that particular spirits, Luciferic spirits, lead up to other principles—*but only to microcosmic principles.* I expressed that earlier when I said:— The Christ is a sort of focal point, in which the Being works through His deed, the Being works through that which He is. Round about the Christ sit the twelve Bodhisattvas of the world, upon whom streams what flows from the Christ, and who elevate it, in the sense of increased wisdom, to higher principles. But it all flows from the fourth principle—even upon the higher principles— insofar as these are evolved on the Earth. On this account there is much error with regard to the uniqueness of the Christ, because there is not a clear understanding that in the Christ we have, to be sure, to do with the fourth principle; but with the fourth *macrocosmic* principle, and even though higher principles can be developed, these are only the *microcosmic* principles of beings who have not come to full development on Old Moon, but who in their way transcend the human. Because they came to unfoldment during the Old Moon evolution, they developed on their part upon the Old Moon what human beings must evolve only upon the Earth.

We must rise to an understanding of such things if we would comprehend the true place of the Christ principle within our Earth evolution, if we would clearly see why the Antichrist will in the future be regarded more highly in many respects than the Christ Himself. The Antichrist will perhaps be found to be more clever, possessed of more genius than the Christ; he will win a powerful following; but spiritual scientists should be prepared in advance, so as not to be deceived by what has now been characterized. More than all else it will be necessary to be firmly established in the good principles of Spiritual Science, in order not to be deceived in this realm. It was the foremost mission of that esotericism which has been developed in the Occident since the 12th century, and about which much has been said, to work out clearly what is to be said about the nature of the Christ in this regard. So that he who is firmly established in this esotericism will recognize more and more clearly that it is a *focal* position which the Christ occupies in the Earth evolution. And concerning all so-called reincarnations of the Christ on our Earth, one can bring forward this quite simple comparison: Just as a balance must be supported at only one point, and not at two or several, so must the Earth evolution have one *basic impulse*. And anyone who admits several incarnations of the Christ makes the same mistake as he who supposes that scales to function properly must be supported in two places. When this is done, they are no longer scales. And anyone who went about on Earth in several incarnations, would no longer be Christ. That is a fact which each well-instructed occultist will urge concerning the nature of Christ. Thus, by a simple comparison we may always point to the uniqueness of the Christ nature; and here the *Gospels* and Spiritual Science are in complete accord.

Notes:

1. Drama of Eduard Schuré: *Die Kinder des Luzifer*. Presented in German by members of the Anthroposophical Society, in the presence of the poet, Munich, 1909 and 1910.

2. Rudolf Steiner, *Occult Physiology*, 1911 (GA 128)

$$\Delta$$

These insights of Rudolf Steiner's into the detailed working of the greatest Avatar of all times, Christ, is instructive in seeing the way Avatars remain with us long after their incarnation or manifestation. A model or copy is left behind in the etheric realm that is perfect and can be multiplied for the use of followers. Christ, as Avatar, also redeemed Earth and renewed its life body or etheric body with the forces He brought down from the spiritual world. These gifts of the greatest Avatar will keep unfolding until the end-of-time as we know it. The Christ Avatar is truly the perfect example of the descent of a god into human incarnation that brought with it everlasting gifts that nourish the soul and elevate the spirit of the aspirant.

Another Avatar that has done a similar thing as the Christ Avatar is the Sophia Avatar. Sophia descended alongside of Christ from the middle ranks of the higher hierarchies. They both descended to Earth and brought heavenly forces with them; Christ brought redemption through love, while Sophia brought Cosmic Wisdom from the ranks of the Kyriotetes (Spirits of Wisdom) with Her. Christ has left a part of His nature called the 'Comforter' (Greek: Paráklētos = English: Paraclete, See: *John* 14:16), or the Holy Spirit. Sophia has left a part of Her nature, called Wisdom, Holy Sophia, or Anthroposophia. This Wisdom of Sophia teaches the true Cosmic nature of Christ's deeds for humanity; it is called, 'Sophia Christos,' or the Wisdom of Christ. Sophia Christos works through the Holy Sophia, who is a close companion and midwife for every aspirant on the path. Just as Christ's Holy Spirit never leaves us, so, too, the Holy Sophia is present for every step gained on the path of spiritual development.

The Kalki Avatar and Maitreya Buddha

This excerpt from *The Gospel of Sophia: The Biographies of the Divine Feminine Trinity*, by Dr. Tyla Gabriel gives us a sweeping picture of the nature of Avatars, bodhisattvas, and buddhas. Dr. Gabriel has a comprehensive grasp of Spiritual Science that includes a profound view of Sophia Christos—the Wisdom of Christ. But Dr. Gabriel also tells us about the tenth incarnation of Vishnu, the Kalki Avatar, who is the female Avatar of our time. The Kalki Avatar comes riding a huge tiger and carrying a flaming sword in her hand to cut off the heads of the ignorant and banish evil. Together with the Maitreya Buddha, the Kalki Avatar focuses on the redemption of the etheric body of the Earth and humanity. Both of these beings work together to prepare humanity for the Second Coming of Christ in the Etheric Realm. Dr. Gabriel tells us:

"There are two streams that help in the process to make sure that humans evolve along at the right pace so that they may return to their rightful homes in heaven. One stream flows down from above. This is Sophia the Daughter and Christ the Son consciously sacrificing themselves and descending from the celestial to the Earthly. This stream of spiritual gifts and guidance happens at the exact right moment in evolution to have the greatest impact on humanity. These gifts are often referred to as gifts or treasures from the Avatars, the lofty spiritual beings who watch over and care for humanity on its road from dark to light. This is the Avatar stream which descends from above.

"The other stream, which ascends from below, is the one that comes from the efforts of humans as they evolve over many incarnations.

"This is often referred to as the path to enlightenment which is known in the East as the vow of the bodhisattva that drives a human to become an enlightened buddha. A bodhisattva is a highly developed initiate who is evolving towards being able to help humanity without having the encumbrance of a human body.

"Gautama Buddha is the most prominent bodhisattva who became a buddha and no longer has to incarnate in a physical body but helps humanity from another realm. Gautama was a human who evolved over many incarnations to reach his Buddhahood. This stream is one that rises up from the Earthly, by human effort, to reach the divine.

"These two streams are found in Sophia the Daughter (Kyriotetes) and Holy Sophia. The Daughter represents the descending stream, and the Holy Sophia represents the ascending stream of spirituality.

"When the Daughter over-lighted Mary, She poured into her spiritual qualities from the paradisiacal realm that renewed her body until it was a virgin, immaculate soul. This was the descending stream of spirit Wisdom from the Beings of Wisdom.

"Eve's efforts throughout many incarnations brought her to the incarnation of Mary where she was able to hold the body of wisdom given to her by Jesus of Nazareth, Earthly wisdom accumulated since the Garden of Eden. From Eve through Mary human development is the ascending, or bodhisattva, stream of spirituality.

"In Mary Sophia we have both streams united, descending and ascending.

"It is little understood that the greatest human initiate is presently the being we have referred to as Mary/Eve/Sophia, Mary Sophia or 'Maria Sophia.'

"The idea that a collective being from the hierarchy of the Beings of Wisdom descended with Christ to the Earth and over-lighted Mary, who was the reincarnation of the original Eve, is almost inconceivable to humans. To add the being of Eve Kadmon, the part of Eve that remained in paradise until she incarnated as Mary of Nazareth, adds a paradox to a mystery. Sophia, the Being of Wisdom, over-lighted Mary/Eve, who was united with Eve Kadmon (Mary of Nazareth who had died when Jesus was twelve), making Mary/Eve the first fully redeemed human being in history. This is the Mary/Eve that is taken bodily into heaven at the Assumption.

"This would seem to make Maria Sophia the most significant human biography that illustrates the future path of all of humanity which will merge the two streams of spirituality, the Avatar and bodhisattva.

"Maria Sophia becomes through her union with her paradisiacal self, one of the first fully realized human being to return to heaven as a prodigal child. Her experience is imprinted in the super-etheric realm around the Earth and available to use by initiates as an aid to their development. And even beyond this marvelous trinity of forces active in Maria Sophia, we also understand that Jesus gave over to Mary his body of wisdom that had ripened the wisdom of Zarathustra, Hermes, and Moses.

"Therefore, Maria Sophia came to hold in her heart the cosmic Wisdom of Sophia and the human wisdom of the great initiates transformed by Jesus.

"This merging of celestial Wisdom given by Sophia and human Earthly wisdom given by Jesus to Mary represents the merging of the two streams of Avatars (celestial) and bodhisattvas (earthly).

"The distinction between heavenly and earthly wisdom is misunderstood by spiritual seekers and more than often the descriptions of Avatars and bodhisattvas are confused by Westerners trying to interpret Eastern doctrines. The mixing of Christian and Buddhist doctrines is a very slippery slope. It is not easy for a western materialist to be able to embody the lofty and celestial ideas concerning the incarnations of Avatars or the nature and work of bodhisattvas.

"The ten incarnations of Vishnu have been taken to be literally true by some western occultists who predict the eminent incarnation of Vishnu as the Kalki Avatar. There are also many people who claim to be the incarnation of the newest bodhisattva who is working to become the next buddha to reach enlightenment—the Maitreya Buddha.

"Avatars descend as perfected beings to bring spiritual manifestations that are needed to sustain humanity on its ascent to the spirit. Bodhisattvas rise-up from human effort into the spiritual world. In Maria Sophia we have the greatest example of the Avatar stream merging with the bodhisattva stream. In Maria Sophia, we have a confluence of beings that was unparalleled.

"Let us look at the greatest of Hindu Avatars, Vishnu, as an illustration of exactly what was meant by that term in the tradition that created it. Vishnu is one of the three gods in the male trinity of the Hindu pantheon. Vishnu is called the sustainer, essentially a similar role as Christ, the second person in the Christian Trinity. He incarnates in a physical form on a regular basis to keep creation in balance. Vishnu has had nine incarnations and his tenth is awaited as the Kalki Avatar.

"Vishnu is the archetypal Avatar who comes from the celestial realm to Earth in whatever form he wishes to take and is not bound by any physical law of nature. He created fantastic wonders during his incarnations. He was there at creation as a giant turtle, then later as a flying boar, then a one-horned whale who saved Manu from the flood, then the half man/ half lion named Narashimha, then the dwarf Vamana who conquered the evil demon Bali, then Parashurama, Rama, Krishna and his brother Balarama.

"The ninth incarnation of Vishnu is hotly debated, some scholars saying Balarama and others saying Gautama Buddha. This debate highlights the confusion between an Avatar and a bodhisattva. Gautama Buddha was clearly a human who evolved to an enlightened state, not an Avatar who descended from heaven. Thus, the debate over the Kalki Avatar began with the enlightenment of Gautama Buddha, and it hasn't ended yet.

"There is another school of thought that believes that when Krishna manifested to Arjuna as his charioteer, this was the tenth incarnation of Vishnu. Some say that this manifestation as Vishu was connected to the descent of Christ into the human realm. Others are convinced that the tenth incarnation of Vishnu as the Kalki Avatar has happened in our own time and that this being has united with the new bodhisattva who is evolving towards becoming the Maitreya Buddha, the successor of the Gautama Buddha.

"The merging of the two streams of Avatars and bodhisattvas is similar to the merging of the celestial and earthly streams that united in Maria Sophia.

"These streams are found also in the divine being of Christ descending into the body of Jesus of Nazareth for three years. Jesus, as a human, then underwent His ministry and passion before He ascended into heaven.

"The veils between all worlds are thinning and humans have one foot on each side of the threshold between the physical and spiritual worlds. Avatars work with bodhisattvas to help them penetrate the veils between these worlds so that they may develop their spiritual nature. But we must be clear about why each tradition has its own version of these spiritual realities and be true to the spirit of current revelation available for the budding bodhisattva in our self.

"The tradition of bodhisattvas is long and involved and is often referred to as the Masters of Wisdom and the Harmony of Feelings and Sensation. This is, in short, what *The Gospel of Sophia* is teaching: the Masters have mastered thinking (wisdom), feeling (harmony of feelings), and willing (harmony of sensations).

"This Great White Brotherhood or Lodge, as it is often called, is traditionally a group of twelve bodhisattvas who are circled around Christ receiving His teachings directly so that they may descend to Earth and share those Wisdom teachings of love with humanity. One bodhisattva at a time comes to the fore and descends into incarnation to bring the teachings of Christ.

"After four or five thousand years, the current bodhisattva then ascends to become a buddha who does not incarnate into a physical body again but rather works from the spiritual world to continue the mission as an ascended master.

"When Gautama Buddha reached enlightenment in a physical body, he chose his successor who is called the Maitreya Buddha, the bringer of good. However, the Maitreya Bodhisattva will not become a buddha for another few thousand years.

"The mission of the Maitreya Buddha is to bring the Wisdom of Christ that illuminates the cosmic nature of Christ's origin and his singular deed that redeemed the Earth and saved it from becoming too hardened and materialized. This is called the Wisdom of Christ, or Sophia of Christ, for it is this Wisdom that will bring understanding about the true nature of Christ's deed and particularly about Christ's redemption and resurrection of the super-etheric body of the Earth and the etheric body of humanity.

"Christ conquered the Earthly realm and now is conquering the etheric realm so that humanity can assume its rightful position in creation. Christ conquered death as an earthly and cosmic "Deed" and this is the message of the Maitreya Buddha in our time.

"When Maitreya speaks, so much wisdom and truth is present in the moral content of the words spoken that they become reality. The Maitreya's words have the power to create, just as the divine spoke creation into being through the Word, or Logos. It is erroneous that the Maitreya Buddha will teach traditional Buddhism. The Maitreya Buddha will teach Christianity in the most profound way.

"Gautama Buddha taught the six steps of compassion that lead to love, but Christ is the author and master of love. Gautama Buddha was intimately involved in the life of Christ and was there from his birth as the Star of Bethlehem. Buddha's higher bodies participated in the Mystery of Golgotha—the life, death, and resurrection of Jesus Christ.

"Buddha was taught by Christ when he was one of the bodhisattvas circled around Him in the spiritual lodge of the Sun. These masters are called many names in many faiths—elders, masters, wise women, bodhisattvas, candles, fires, and other such names.

"In our times, due to the incarnation of Ahriman, the great deceiver and father of lies, both groups of twelve circled around Christ are currently active on the Earth. This is the first time that such a dramatic event as this has happened. All twenty-four elders, plus Avatars, bodhisattvas, arahants, mahatmas, saints, patriarchs, and a host of other great spiritual beings are incarnating at this time. This is well known by clairvoyants in these traditions who can witness such events. This is an unprecedented time that is a fulcrum of evolution. The battle between light and dark is raging and human evolution is at a precipice.

"One of the reasons that so many great spiritual beings have incarnated to wage the battle against materialism and the forces of Ahriman, and his followers is because human bodies have degraded so much that it is very difficult for spiritual beings to find suitable human bodies that can carry the weight of spiritual consciousness in these hyper-materialistic times. Many great beings are finding bodies that do not permit them to manifest their spiritual strength without great hindrances.

"Thus, of the twenty-four elders it will be hard to find twelve who can join together to confront the incarnation of Ahriman and the many dark beings who have also taken form with him. Without the lodge of the elders working to bring light and warmth into the grey shadow-thoughts of materialism that have become common in the world, much of humanity will fail to evolve properly and move forward in evolution. The battle for humanity is being waged day and night and most people have no idea of the costs. Humans will either become angels or animals and the Avatars and bodhisattvas are committed to serve the angelic in humans.

"Avatars and bodhisattvas, the celestial and the earthly, hang in the balance of what humans will do in these crucial years of trying to keep the spiritual world from darkening our consciousness. When a materialist sleeps or dies, he does not have spiritual food to feed the spiritual hierarchy and thus the spiritual world has no food to feed him. Subsequently light is not born and all is turned towards darkness in both realms. Christ is crucified again in the etheric realm of light and life by dark materialistic thinking.

"Humans are starving from the lack of spiritual nourishment because they bring none to the spiritual world. As a result, human evolution could be lost to evil beings who want to impede and end human spiritual development. This death of the spirit has caused the spiritual world to empty itself of souls and flood the Earth with as much help as it can send.

"We need to remember that Sophia is higher than an Avatar and is ready to help the bodhisattva in us blossom into the spiritual world. Sophia as Maria Sophia is far beyond a bodhisattva who evolves into a buddha. She is a perfect archetype to emulate as she is a balance between celestial and earthly.

"Christ is the Being we all must meet each time we cross the threshold between the physical and spiritual worlds. Currently, we have the greatest help from the spiritual world that can be imagined. All around us are the great spiritual teachers of all time, incarnated to help us move along the spiritual path of self-development. We should remember that any spiritual being can alight in our spirit, even if for only a moment of golden illumination.

"We need to take the vow of the bodhisattva, which is, that we will continue to strive towards enlightenment for the sake of all other sentient beings. This is a pre-requisite for advancing towards our Buddhahood or Christened Self.

"The author points to Hindu tradition to be most helpful and accurate—that the Kalki Avatar will be the incarnation of Kali herself. The Hindu text *Divya Maha Kala Jnana* (*The Divine Knowledge of Time*), written around 1000 AD by Jagas Guru Srimad Virat Potaluru Veera Brahmendra Maha Swami, describes social conditions before the arrival of Kali Purusha, the Kalki Avatar, by the Kali year 5101 (1999 AD).

"This being, it is told, is the incarnation of Kali, the destructive and procreative female aspect of the divine. It is predicted that Kali Purusha will be called Sree Sree Sree ("Thrice Great") Veera Bhoga Vasataraya Maha Swami and will carry a fiery sword to strike off the head of ignorance and champion Wisdom.

"The Divine Feminine Trinity is a similar archetype to this prediction of the Thrice Great Goddess, who is the necessary spiritual teacher or Avatar of our times.

"The forces of Kali are the forces of death that accompany her consort, Shiva. It is the feminine forces of death that also create the forces of birth, that are needed to overcome the deadening forces of materialism that threaten to destroy humanity's opportunity for spiritual advancement in this age of hyper-materialism.

"The Maitreya Buddha is like the Holy Sophia as She slowly develops Herself and humanity in the process of spiritual evolution from the Earth to the realm of Queen of Heaven.

"The Holy Sophia knows the suffering and strife of human life and is there to help midwife all of our efforts to birth the spirit. Like a bodhisattva, She has taken the vow to help all humans embody their angelic self and enter the super-etheric realm of the divine. Surely Sophia, in Her many forms, changes into the very companion we need to make the journey to our higher self."

Cult of the Personality or Guru Devotion?

Anthroposophists (students of Rudolf Steiner's teachings) have often been accused of developing a cult of personality to enshrine Rudolf Steiner in saintly or mythological icons that are divorced of human inadequacies, unspiritual personality characteristics, and vices. Some shrines to Rudolf Steiner are the second Goetheanum (the building that houses the world headquarters of the Anthroposophical Society) Waldorf schools throughout the world, Christian Community churches, Anthroposophical medical facilities, bio-dynamic farms worldwide, and many other educational and social endeavors. Often, the people working in these institutions are only slightly acquainted with the teachings of Rudolf Steiner and thus lead somewhat hypocritical lives supporting a man and a cause that they personally cannot justify. When a co-worker in an Anthroposophical institution is asked why they 'follow' a man who was a racist, a sexist, a fascist who taught crazy things about demons named Lucifer, Ahriman, and Sorath, and clairvoyantly 'reads from the Akashic Chronicles' histories of Atlantis, Lemuria, and other more ancient cultures—they don't know what to say. Usually, a parroted answer they heard from an older Anthroposophist comes immediately to their mouth and they find themselves saying things they truly don't understand. Anthroposophists are in a 'school' of spiritual development that leads to 'etheric vision' or clairvoyance. Unfortunately, most followers of

Rudolf Steiner are not clairvoyant and even though they might have spent a lifetime practicing Rudolf Steiner's spiritual exercises, all they have left at the end of the day is to quote Rudolf Steiner or read more of his books that describe the spiritual world the aspirant is longing for. This usually ends in devotion to Rudolf Steiner and another vote for his spiritual canonization.

'Saint Rudolf' becomes the bottom line for most true believers in Rudolf Steiner who sincerely try the exercises but don't get clairvoyant results. A school for clairvoyance devoid of clairvoyant results doesn't work well. This is a true embarrassment for the Anthroposophical Society. Often, anyone claiming clairvoyance makes a big splash in the Anthroposophic networks and institutions and their presence usually creates a schism of those who believe the clairvoyant and those who don't. This pattern started even before Rudolf Steiner's funeral. Factions arose and the Anthroposophical Society split, again and again. Nearly a century after Rudolf Steiner's death, no apparent spiritual successor to Rudolf Steiner has arisen, even though we have seen many people claim to be the reincarnation of Rudolf Steiner or one of the other highly developed people who Rudolf Steiner spoke about. Saint Rudolf is dead—but his followers surge forward believing they are doing Rudolf Steiner's work on the Earth or that they are one of the only people on the Earth who 'understands' Saint Rudolf, or in fact, they are Saint Rudolf reincarnated.

All of these sad and pathetic soul dysfunctions are completely understandable when we reflect upon the fact that Rudolf Steiner died in 1925 and appointed no single successor. This was tragic for the Anthroposophical Society because it effectively became a 'cult of personality' for a dead man. Usually, the cult of personality bolsters the image of a living leader who needs to stay in power and progress in his image to that of a saint who is divinely inspired and chosen to lead the lesser humans beneath him. Just as Caesar went from man to god through a political cult of personality, so too, modern spiritual teachers are deified after their death and the unseemly aspects of the personality white-washed while a golden crown, or halo, is bestowed by higher spiritual beings upon their sacred brow. This practice of blatantly brandishing a cult of personality on a living dictator is laughed at in the West but it is still practiced all over the globe to this day. It is effective and though seemingly stupid and an obvious lie—blazing an icon into the subconscious eventually wears its way into the soul. After a while, building-high pictures of dictators instill fear that eventually becomes comfort and security. The evil omnipotent dad becomes the loving omnipresent father all too easy.

Since Saint Rudolf is dead and no successors have been adopted by the Anthroposophical Society—it is a ship without a captain, and no one is at the helm. Perhaps if the hypnotic glaze over the eyes of followers were lifted for a moment, it would be obvious that the cult of personality has been placed on a dead man. It won't work. Who do the Anthroposophists think they are trying to kid? What is the point of worshiping Saint Rudolf if there are no successors to lead the Society? Thus, the Society is filled with hypocrites who want to be 'like' Saint Rudolf; but there is no one in the Anthroposophic Society who could tell a follower whether or not their 'spiritual development' is true or false. There can be no more saints in Anthroposophy because Anthroposophists will just argue over who is clairvoyant and who is not. Otherwise, non-clairvoyant students study Saint Rudolf's teachings; but they don't know for sure if what they think Saint Rudolf said is actually true. Anthroposophists argue over everything Saint Rudolf said. Everyone has their own version of Saint Rudolf's teachings and they overlay whatever spiritual perspective, no matter how limited, on top of that confused mess of thoughts, and some followers just spit out whatever fantasy comes into their mind under the auspices of 'spiritual research.'

Some critics of Steinerites believe that the followers usually have problems with father figures, authority, and convention. These problems with submission to authority demand that Saint Rudolf must be bronzed and canonized, thereby keeping him quiet and only used as an authority to authenticate some personal belief or lifestyle. Followers can't speak with a living teacher and get personal direction. Rudolf himself tells his followers that he was initiated by a Master; but they will have to undergo initiation on their own and without any physical Master beings. This is convenient for followers because they are essentially 'on their own' with no one to correct them or tell them they have to do any spiritual work they don't like. With a dead spiritual teacher, it becomes a smorgasbord of spiritual delights that are chosen through the caprice of the student. No real work is required to be a follower, just parroting the standard dogma and attitudes will do quite nicely. No tests will be given to determine just how much of Saint Rudolf you have read and understood. Pretty much, followers of a dead teacher are free to do as they please and yet get to subsume the 'initiate' level of their teacher—who loves them from beyond the grave—even if their own father didn't. An adopted spiritual dad is wonderful to have while romping through the Grail 'Castle of Marvels.' (Château des Merveilles) You really can't go wrong—or can you?

Unfortunately, the cult of personality is confused with the Tibetan practice of Guru Devotion. Again, even guru devotion should be practiced on a living Master to be most effective, and perhaps in Saint Rudolf's day it was the cause for so much devotion to him. In the practice of guru devotion, the student is supposed to look everywhere they can to find the best teacher available. Once a teacher is found, it is the responsibility of the student to plumb the faults and foibles of the guru trying to unmask any 'sins' or shortcomings that might exist. Any and all questions are allowed, and the guru's responses should inform the student whether the student can accept the guru as a human who is evolving and ascending; but yet, may still have a dark side to transform. If the guru were perfect, he would simply ascend. If the guru is on the Earth, they have a dark side yet to be transformed. That is why it is incumbent upon the student to find the very best model of perfection that they can. It is essential in these guru devotion practices to find a living teacher so that the teacher can be tested to see if the student can use the guru as a spiritual model to emulate. Guru devotion is like deity worship in its first stages. The student learns to follow, mimic, or emulate the guru and this will take the student the next steps on the gradual path of ascension.

Once the guru is chosen by the student, there can be no more questioning of the guru's personal faults or shortcomings. As a matter of fact, the more the student looks for the faults of the guru after the student has made the choice, the more the student's spiritual practice is doomed to fail through the instruction of that particular guru. Idolizing the guru enhances spiritual advancement. The more the student can see the "higher self" of the guru, the more they can see their own higher self. It is directly proportional. Therefore, the guru becomes the representation of the spiritual in this domain and the more devoted and dedicated the student is to the guru, the more potential the student has to attain the same level of spiritual development as the guru. First, the student becomes 'identified' with the guru through the selection process and the ensuing devotion—a type of imitation. Second, the student gives over all 'authority' to the guru and completely trusts and obeys everything they do and say. This is a type of 'authority' worship. The student no longer has to trust his own inspiration but can rely on the teacher's inspiration and connection to the spiritual world. Third, the student tries in every way to 'embody' the guru and become what they are. The student attempts to be become 'one' with the guru.

Unfortunately, there are negative aspects of guru devotion since it is no longer a viable path to the spirit in the modern world. Distortions of the cult of personality and elements of guru devotion have devolved into their dark side due to misplaced spiritual practices. The chart below illustrates what becomes of misplaced identification, surrendering of authority, and false embodiment of the guru's model.

Identification	Thinking	Imagination
Over-identification	Surrenders thinking	Relying on the teacher
Fantasy taken as real	Anti-Imagination	Pride and Sloth
Astral forces of Lucifer	Occult lies	Doubt

This first stage is simply a desire to 'be like the guru' that has gone wrong and stolen the forces of Imagination and turned them into the un-imaginative idea of sitting back and letting the teacher do the work. Then, when the student identifies with this body of spiritual teaching, they become inappropriately prideful of this work which they did not accomplish on their own. This is lazy spiritual practice. Just identify with the teacher, and then quote him whenever necessary making sure to take the full credit yourself for being equal to the thought. Fantasizing with the ideas of the teacher may harm the student. Spiritual credit is only given for work the individual has done, not the work of their teacher. Lucifer abounds in these realms and tells the student that they are equal to the teacher, since they can think their thoughts. This leads to the personal 'occult lie' that the student can assume the mantle of the teacher without work. Imitation is a good beginning; but at some point, the student must stand alone. Standing with the teacher's ideas as your own can lead to a total 'crash' of thinking wherein doubt fills the soul. Or the opposite can happen when a maniac desire to convince the world that your teacher is correct can drive the student—thus making the student feel more 'correct' all the time. Then, over-identification with the teacher takes control of the student.

Authority	Feeling	Inspiration
Obsession	Surrenders feeling	Infallible teacher
Fascination	Anti-Inspiration	Envy and Greed
Ahriman	Occult Imprisonment	Hatred

The second stage builds upon the former and takes the manic drive to be 'like' the teacher into an unhealthy obsession with the teacher and the teachings. The student can become filled with the teachings and yet not have the resultant clairvoyance and therefore falls back on the intellect instead of moving into loving thoughts. This obsession with 'being right' because the teacher 'said so' is the bane of Anthroposophists. They become cold-hearted in their lonely ivory towers of correctness due to their superlative ability to 'quote' the teachings and seemingly 'own' the teachings. These ahrimanically inspired students quote words that have not been digested through personal experience—thus, becoming a force that slays the soul and spirit. Pretty soon, the alienated student hates all others who do not interpret the teacher's words the way they do. Fights ensue and the battle for 'king of the hill' never ends. Opinions are proffered and the different schools of thought, or battle encampments, are built and defended. Enemies are developed and schisms abound. Vicious attacks on others are justified because one believes the other has defiled the beloved teacher's holy teachings. Little or no inspiration comes from the self-appointed defenders of the faith and anti-social behavior is used like weapons. Dead, cold thoughts are the outcome of the battles where a lack of Inspiration is found on both sides. Envy starts the process and greed makes sure it never ends. Eventually, fascination sets in like a hypnotic trance and the fighters even forget what they are fighting about—but the battle wages on. In its worst case, the student becomes imprisoned by their own illusions. This is called occult imprisonment, which is self-made and very hard to free oneself from.

Embodiment	Willing	Intuition
Possession	Surrenders willing	Believing they are the teacher
Fabrication fills the ego	Anti-Intuition	Lust and Gluttony
Forces of the Asuras	Occult Illness	Fear

The third stage can be experienced without either of the two preceding stages but sometimes follows in sequence. Often, mentally ill people are drawn to spiritual paths. These people may not go through the first two stages to attain the third. In the case where the student has gone through the first two stages, embodiment is the next logical step after over-identification and surrendering of authority. Embodiment is like the Rosicrucian stages of spiritual development where the student personally experiences the physical passion of Christ as an Imitation of His life and death. This becomes a physical experience in the soul. When it is done improperly, in relationship to the chosen teacher, it can lead to delusion and psychosis wherein the student actually believes they are the reincarnated teacher or some other great being. Of course, it would seem to any sane person that the student is not the teacher literally—as in reincarnation. This fantasy, delusion, and occult imprisonment is very serious and often leads to needing psychiatric treatment. Most anyone will see that the delusional student is 'crazy' quite quickly but the student himself will not see the gross psychosis. Crazy people don't know they are crazy. It is sad but it is to be expected that a great light like Rudolf Steiner would naturally cast many a dark shadow in his students who wish to canonize, deify, or 'go beyond' the beloved teacher. Often, the gross pride, envy, lust, greed, sloth, and gluttony of the student is completely denied and cannot be seen or acknowledged by the student. This is because the student has incorrectly used guru devotion to develop an evil 'double' of the teachings and now, through their delusion and psychosis, have defiled the teachings in a most materialistic way. Soon, the fabrications and confabulations of the deluded student are spread abroad with anti-intuitions that often don't agree with the teacher and attempt to 'go beyond' the teacher—who is conveniently dead and can't respond to the insult. This type of occult imprisonment leads to occult illness that feeds the Asuras who consume parts of the ego of the deluded student. This is lust and gluttony at its worst because the parts of the ego lost in the process cannot be gained back, they are lost to personal spiritual development. Megalomania is the usual outcome.

One might ask, what is the way around these problems and how are they to be avoided? It is really quite simple. In spiritual practice it is very important to dedicate all of your spiritual efforts to the advancement of all other beings. Yes, your personal self-development must be for the sake of all others. This may seem like an oxymoron; but it is true. In Tibetan Buddhism, it is called 'dedicating the merit.' In this practice, after each session of meditation or spiritual practice the very merit, or good, that has come from the spiritual effort is offered up to the beings above the individual's crown chakra. The aspirant bundles up all of the good and gives it over to all others in a field called the 'illusory body.' This body carries and protects the spiritual efforts of the aspirant against the 'sins' that may cause the aspirant to fall back into a less spiritual condition. Anger and other deadly sins destroy the merit of spiritual effort if this merit is not protected in a place that personal vice cannot get to it. Spiritual merit is like love, it must be given away. You can't store love and you should not try to personally store spiritual merit within the personal aura. If you do not 'give away' your spiritual merit, it can haunt you and eventually obsess and possess the soul and spirit and become a hindrance to advancement. Also, you can lose all of it by fits of anger or unkind deeds. This is what happens to the delusional person who believes they physically embody the dead teacher. They are personally attached to their supposed spiritual understanding and advancement which builds an occult prison for them. It is like a hall of mirrors where everything is the personal self which is projected into infinity.

It is worth our spiritual effort to be aware of the preceding anti-steps in spiritual development. These steps are very common and need the objectivity of others to shine a proper light on as to whether we have fallen prey to the shadow side of Imagination, Inspiration, and Intuition or whether our efforts are benefiting others. One sure way to know is to simply ask the question of yourself: Who am I doing my spiritual work for; myself or others? Christ will fill you with the answer that you do all spiritual work for the 'Christ in others' rather than the luciferic spirit within yourself. Lucifer may shine brighter and build the ego quicker; but that ego is built on shifting sands. Christ's presence is always centered on serving others, not the selfish lower self. The ultimate teacher is Christ Himself and all other teachers are subordinate.

Anthroposophists need to recognize Rudolf Steiner's teachings objectively and weigh them against the eternal truths that exist in every striving student of Spiritual Science and then the negative forces of the cult of personality and guru devotion can be overcome.

BIBLIOGRAPHY

- Andreæ, Johann Valentin. *Reipublicæ Christianopolitanæ descriptio*. Argentorati: Sumptibus hæredum Lazari Zetzneri, Strasbourg, 1619.

- Andreæ, Johann Valentin. *Johann Valentin Andreae's Christianopolis; an ideal state of the seventeenth century*. translated from the Latin of Johann Valentin Andreae with an historical introduction. by Felix Emil Held. The Graduate School of the University of Illinois, Urbana- Champaign, 1916.

- Arnold, Edwin Sir. *The Light of Asia, or The Great Renunciation (Mahâbhinishkramana): Being the Life and Teaching Gautama, Prince of India and Founder of Buddhism (As Told in Verse by an Indian Buddhist)*. Kegan Paul, Trench, Trübner & Co., London, 1879.

- Avari, Burjor. *India: The Ancient Past: A History of the Indian Sub-Continent*. Routledge, New Edition, 2007.

- Barnwell, John. *The Arcana of the Grail Angel: The Spiritual Science of the Holy Blood and of the Holy Grail*. Verticordia Press, Bloomfield Hills, 1999.

- Barnwell, John. *The Arcana of Light on the Path: The Star Wisdom of the Tarot and Light on the Path*. Verticordia Press, Bloomfield Hills, 1999.

- Blavatsky, H. P. (Helena Petrovna). *Isis Unveiled: A Master-Key to the Mysteries of Ancient and Modern Science and Theology*. J. W. Bouton. New York, 1878.

243

- Blavatsky, H. P. (Helena Petrovna). *The Key to Theosophy: Being a Clear Exposition, in the Form of Question and Answer, of the Ethics, Science and Philosophy for the Study of Which the Theosophical Society Has Been Founded.* The Theosophical Publishing Company, Ltd. London, 1889.

- Blavatsky, H. P. (Helena Petrovna). *The Secret Doctrine: The Synthesis of Science, Religion and Philosophy.* The Theosophical Publishing Company, Ltd. London, 1888.

- Blavatsky, H. P. (Helena Petrovna). *The Voice of Silence: Being Extracts from the Book of the Golden Precepts.* Theosophical University Press, 1992.

- Bockemuhl, Jochen. *Toward a Phenomenology of the Etheric World: Investigations into the Life of Nature and Man.* Anthroposophic Press, Spring Valley, N. Y., 1977.

- Campanella, Tommaso. *The City of the Sun.* The ProjectGutenberg Ebook, David Widger, 2013.

- Colum, Padriac. *Orpheus: Myths of the World.* Floris Books. Colum, Padriac. The Children's Homer. MacMillan Co., 1946.

- Colum, Padriac. *The Tales of Ancient Egypt.* Henry Walck Incorporated, New York,1968.

- Crawford, John Martin. *The Kalevala: The Epic Poem of Finland.* John B. Alden, New York, 1888.

- Gabriel, Douglas. *The Eternal Curriculum for Wisdom Children: Intuitive Learning and the Etheric Body.* Our Spirit, Northville, 2017.

- Gabriel, Tyla. *The Gospel of Sophia: The Biographies of the Divine Feminine Trinity,* Volume Our Spirit, Northville, 2014.

- Gabriel, Tyla. *The Gospel of Sophia: A Modern Path of Initiation,* Volume 2. Our Spirit, Northville, 2015.

- Gabriel, Tyla and Douglas. *The Gospel of Sophia: Sophia Christos Initiation,* Volume 3. Our Spirit, Northville, 2016.

- Gabriel, Douglas. *The Spirit of Childhood.* Trinosophia Press, Berkley, 1993.

- Gabriel, Douglas. *The Eternal Ethers: A Theory of Everything.* Our Spirit, Northville, 2018.

- Gabriel, Douglas. *Goddess Meditations.* Trinosophia Press, Berkley, 1994.

- Gebser, Jean. *The Ever Present Origin.* Ohio University Press, 1991.

- Green, Roger Lancelyn & Heather Copley. *Tales of Ancient Egypt.* Puffin Books, New York, 1980.

- Harrison, C. G. *The Transcendental Universe; Six Lectures on Occult Science, Theosophy, and the Catholic Faith.* George Redway, London 1893.

- Harrison, C. G. *The Transcendental Universe; Six Lectures on Occult Science, Theosophy, and the Catholic Faith.* Delivered Before the Berean Society, edited with an introduction by Christopher Bamford. Lindesfarne Press, Hudson, 1993.

- Hamilton, Edith. *Mythology.* Little Brown And Co., Boston, 1942.

- Harrer, Dorothy. *Chapters from Ancient History.* Waldorf Publications, Chatham, 2016.

- Hazeltine, Alice Isabel. *Hero Tales from Many Lands.* Abingdon Press, New York, 1961.

- Heidel, Alexander. *The Babylonian Genesis: The Story of Creation*. University of Chicago Press, Chicago, 1942.

- Hiebel, Frederick. *The Gospel of Hellas*. Anthroposophic Press, New York, 1949.

- Jocelyn, Beredene. *Citizens of the Cosmos: Life's Unfolding from Conception through Death to Rebirth*. Continuum, New York, 1981.

- König, Karl. *Earth and Man*. Bio-Dynamic Literature, Wyoming, Rhode Island, 1982.

- Kovacs, Charles. *Ancient Mythologies and History*. Resource Books, Scotland, 1991.

- Kovacs, Charles. *Greek Mythology and History*. Resource Books, Scotland, 1991.

- Landscheidt, Theodor. *Sun-Earth-Man a Mesh of Cosmic Oscillations: How Planets Regulate Solar Eruptions, Geomagnetic Storms, Conditions of Life, and Economic Cycles*. Urania Trust, London, 1989.

- Laszlo, Ervin and Kingsley, Dennis L. *Dawn of the Akashic Age: New Consciousness, Quantum Resonance, and the Future of the World*. Inner Traditions, Rochester Vermont, 2013

- Plato. *The Republic*. Dover Thrift Editions, 2000.

- Sister Nivedita (Margaret E. Noble) & Coomaraswamy, Ananda K.. *Myths of the Hindus and Buddhists*. Henry Holt, New York 1914.

- Rudolf Steiner, Rudolf. *Ancient Myths: Their Meaning and Connection with Evolution*. Rudolf Steiner Book Center, 1971.

- Rudolf Steiner, Rudolf. *Christ and the Spiritual World: The Search for the Holy Grail*. Rudolf Steiner Press, London, 1963.

- Rudolf Steiner, Rudolf. *Foundations of Esotericism*. Rudolf Steiner Press, London, 1983.

- Rudolf Steiner, Rudolf. *Isis Mary Sophia: Her Mission and Ours*. Rudolf Steiner Books, 2003.

- Rudolf Steiner, Rudolf. *Man as a Being of Sense and Perception*. Rudolf Steiner Book Center, Vancouver, 1981.

- Rudolf Steiner, Rudolf. *Man as Symphony of the Creative Word*. Rudolf Steiner Publishing, London, 1978.

- Rudolf Steiner, Rudolf. *Occult Science*. Anthroposophic Press, NY, 1972.

- Rudolf *Steiner, Rudolf. Rosicrucian Esotericism. Anthroposophic Press, NY,* 1978.

- Rudolf Steiner, Rudolf. *Rosicrucian Wisdom: An Introduction*. Rudolf Steiner Press, London, 2000. GA 425

- Rudolf Steiner, Rudolf. *The Bridge between Universal Spirituality and the Physical Constitution of Man*. Anthroposophic Press, NY, 1958.

ABOUT
DR. RUDOLF STEINER

Rudolf Steiner was born on the 27th of February 1861 in Kraljevec in the former Kingdom of Hungary and now Croatia. He studied at the College of Technology in Vienna and obtained hisdoctorate at the University of Rostock with a dissertation on Theory of Knowledge which concluded with the sentence: "The most important problem of human thinking is this: to understand the human being as a free personality, whose very foundation is himself."

He exchanged views widely with the personalities involved in cultural life and arts of his time. However, unlike them, he experienced the spiritual realm as the other side of reality. He gained access through exploration of consciousness using the same method as the natural scientist uses for the visible world in his external research. This widened perspective enabled him to give significant impulses in many areas such as art, pedagogy, curative education, medicine, agriculture, architecture, economics, and social sciences, aiming towards the spiritual renewal of civilization.

He gave his movement the name of "Anthroposophy" (the wisdom of humanity) after separating from the German section of the Theosophical Society, where he had acted as a general secretary. He then founded the Anthroposophical Society in 1913 which formed its center with the construction of the First Goetheanum in Dornach, Switzerland. Rudolf Steiner died on 30th March 1925 in Dornach. His literary work is made up of numerous books, transcripts and approximately 6000 lectures which have for the most part been edited and published in the Complete Works Edition.

Steiner's basic books, which were previously a prerequisite to gaining access to his lectures, are: *Theosophy, The Philosophy of Freedom, How to Know Higher Worlds, Christianity as a Mystical Fact,* and *Occult Science.*

ABOUT THE AUTHOR, DR. DOUGLAS GABRIEL

Dr. Gabriel is a retired superintendent of schools and professor of education who has worked with schools and organizations throughout the world. He has authored many books ranging from teacher training manuals to philosophical/spiritual works on the nature of the divine feminine.

He was a Waldorf class teacher and administrator at the Detroit Waldorf School and taught courses at Mercy College, the University of Detroit, and Wayne State University for decades. He then became the Headmaster of a Waldorf School in Hawaii and taught at the University of Hawaii, Hilo. He was a leader in the development of charter schools in Michigan and helped found the first Waldorf School in the Detroit Public School system and the first charter Waldorf School in Michigan.

Gabriel received his first degree in religious formation at the same time as an associate degree in computer science in 1972. This odd mixture of technology and religion continued throughout his life. He was drafted into and served in the Army Security Agency (NSA) where he was a cryptologist and systems analyst in signal intelligence, earning him a degree in signal broadcasting. After military service, he entered the Catholic Church again as a Trappist monk and later as a Jesuit priest where he earned PhD's in philosophy and comparative religion, and a Doctor of Divinity. As a Jesuit priest, he came to Detroit and earned a BA in anthroposophical studies and history and a MA in school administration. Gabriel left the priesthood and became a Waldorf class teacher and administrator in Detroit and later in Hilo, Hawaii.

Douglas has been a sought-after lecturer and consultant to schools and businesses throughout the world and in 1982 he founded the Waldorf Educational Foundation that provides funding for the publication of educational books. He has raised a great deal of money for Waldorf schools and institutions that continue to develop the teachings of Dr. Rudolf Steiner. Douglas is now retired but continues to write a variety of books including a novel and a science fiction thriller. He has four children, who keep him busy and active and a wife who is always striving towards the spirit through creating an "art of life." She is the author of the *Gospel of Sophia* trilogy.

The Gabriels' articles, blogs, and videos can currently be found at:

OurSpirit.com
Neoanthroposphy.com
GospelofSophia.com
EternalCurriculum.com

TRANSLATOR'S NOTE

The Rudolf Steiner quotes in this book can be found, in most cases, in their full-length and in context, through the Rudolf Steiner Archives by an Internet search of the references provided. We present the quoted selections of Rudolf Steiner from a free rendered translation of the original while utilizing comparisons of numerous German to English translations that are available from a variety of publishers and other sources. In some cases, the quoted selections may be condensed and partially summarized using the same, or similar in meaning, words found in the original. Brackets are used to insert [from the author] clarifying details or anthroposophical nomenclature and spiritual scientific terms.

We chose to use GA (Gesamtausgabe—collected edition) numbers to reference Rudolf Steiner's works instead of CW (Collected Works), which is often used in English editions. Some books in the series, *From the Works of Rudolf Steiner*, have consciously chosen to use a predominance of Rudolf Steiner quotes to drive the presentation of the themes rather than personal remarks and commentary.

We feel that Rudolf Steiner's descriptions should not be truncated but need to be translated into an easily read format for the English-speaking reader, especially for those new to Anthroposophy. We recommend that serious aspirants read the entire lecture, or chapter, from which the Rudolf Steiner quotation was taken, because nothing can replace Rudolf Steiner's original words or the mood in which they were delivered. The style of speaking and writing has changed dramatically over the last century and needs updating in style and presentation to translate into a useful tool for spiritual study in modern times. The series, *From the Works of Rudolf Steiner* intends to present numerous "study guides" for the beginning aspirant, and the initiate, in a format that helps support the spiritual scientific research of the reader.

Printed in Great Britain
by Amazon

51422260R00145